Gift
of
CBS

FOOL OF
LOVE

FOOL
OF
LOVE

THE LIFE OF RAMON LULL

E. ALLISON PEERS

22123

S. C. M. PRESS LIMITED
56 BLOOMSBURY ST., LONDON, W.C.1

TO JORDI RUBIÓ,
Through bad times and good,
devoted Lullist
and
devoted friend.

First published September 1946

Distributed in Canada by our exclusive agents
The Macmillan Company of Canada Limited
70 Bond Street, Toronto

PRINTED IN GREAT BRITAIN BY
NORTHUMBERLAND PRESS LIMITED
GATESHEAD ON TYNE

CONTENTS

PRINCIPAL ABBREVIATIONS

R.L.   E. ALLISON PEERS: *Ramon Lull, a Biography*. London. S.P.C.K. 1929

B.B.   *The Book of the Beasts*. London. Burns Oates and Washbourne. 1927

B.L.B. *The Book of the Lover and the Beloved*. New edition. London. S.P.C.K. 1946 (*Note:* The footnote references are to this edition, or to the edition incorporated in *Blanquerna*, and not to the original edition of 1923.)

Bl.   *Blanquerna*. London. Jarrolds. 1926

C.B.   (" Contemporary Biography ": Cf. p. 12) *A Life of Ramon Lull*. London. Burns Oates and Washbourne. 1927

T.L.   *The Tree of Love*. London. S.P.C.K. 1926

FOREWORD

IF THE TEACHING of St. John of the Cross, which I described in *Spirit of Flame*, was found invigorating in days of crisis, when faith burned low and men's hearts were failing them for fear, the vital and compelling personality of the Majorcan, Ramon Lull, should be no less of an inspiration at a time when the watchwords of the world are Reconstruction, Advance and Progress.

The Fool of Love, as he delighted to call himself, lived in the thirteenth century, but so skilfully has recent scholarship divested his biography of the accretions of age that the portrait it enables me to present is uncannily modern. I have drawn it only in outline, so that its essentials may stand out the more clearly; but, though these pages are not burdened with footnotes, they contain enough references to the few works of Lull's which have been translated into English to permit of further study by those who wish to know him better.

By the courtesy of the S.P.C.K. I have drawn freely upon my *Ramon Lull, a Biography*, published shortly before the seven-hundredth anniversary of Ramon's birth. Where limits of space have imposed undue condensation I have added footnote references to that ampler study, in which fuller details of all kinds and an adequate bibliography of Lullian literature will also be found.

E.A.P.

UNIVERSITY OF LIVERPOOL
JULY 1, 1945

I desire to be a fool

that I may give honour and glory

to God, and

I will have no art nor device

in my words

by reason of the greatness

of my love

Blanquerna, Chapter 79

I

VISION INTO ACTION

*The Beloved revealed Himself to His Lover,
clothed in new and scarlet robes. He stretched
out His arms to embrace him; He inclined His
head to kiss him; and He remained on high
that he might ever seek Him.* —B.L.B., 91

IT WAS A SUMMER EVENING in Majorca in the year
1263—and summer evenings in Majorca are apt to be torrid.
But the faintest breeze was coming in from the Mediterranean and stirring the hair of the young man as he sat
intently over something he was writing on a sheet of paper.
Anyone watching him for a time might well have wondered
what he was doing. Absorbed in his work though he was—
and it was characteristic of him to be absorbed in what he
did: he never did things by halves—he would stop now and
again, raise his eyes from his paper, stare fixedly into space
and abstractedly hum a bar or two of a popular air before
returning to a feverish bout of scribbling. He was a hand-
some young man, fashionably dressed, with more than a
suggestion about him of gay living. Not at all the sort of
man whom one would have credited with such capacity for
concentration—especially, in those unliterary days, for concentration on a piece of writing.

His name was Ramon Lull and he had not long since
been keeping his thirtieth birthday. His father, now dead,
had been a man of good position in Barcelona, who had
sailed in the armada led by the young King of Catalonia-

9

Aragon, afterwards known as King James the Conqueror, on the expedition which captured the island of Majorca from the pugnacious Moors. With one of his brothers, he decided to settle in the newly won island, so he brought his young wife from the mainland, and bought a house in Palma, where very soon afterwards his only son was born.

Land was cheap in Majorca and Ramon's father acquired it in some quantity, no doubt with the intention of founding one of the leading Majorcan families of the future. Ramon was educated with the care befitting a boy of good lineage. He was apparently intended to be a courtier, for at the age of fourteen he entered the King's service as a page and became the companion of his two sons, Peter and James. When James reached school age, Ramon, who was about ten years his senior, was appointed his tutor, and there sprang up between them a friendship which the practically-minded young man was later able to turn to good account.

In the summer of the year 1256, the Conqueror made it known that his son James would, in due time, be created King of Majorca, and Ramon, being a Majorcan by birth, accompanied him on a visit to his future realm. Soon afterwards he began to travel more widely—either in the company of the King, as his seneschal, or on his service. All over the rapidly extending kingdom of Catalonia-Aragon he went—beyond what is now the French frontier, to Perpignan and Montpellier; to Corbeil, for the betrothal of the Princess Elizabeth to the son of St. Louis; and into Castile, with whose King the Conqueror maintained a politic friendship.

These travels did much to broaden Ramon's experience. His easy and genial disposition would certainly have made him welcome wherever he went. But, thorough as he always was in whatever he did, he evidently had too little to do, and the pleasant life he led proved demoralizing. As he grew into manhood, he showed every sign of becoming a dissolute courtier. " The more apt I found myself to sin," he wrote of himself, " the more I allowed my nature to obey the dictates of my body."[1] He married, it is true, probably while he was with Prince James in Majorca : some think that the marriage was arranged by the Prince himself, and that he was seeking, in a way characteristic of his gentle temperament, to reform him. But neither his marriage, nor the subsequent birth to him of a son and a daughter, sufficed to check his unruly passions. " The beauty of women ", he wrote of this period ten years later, was " a plague and tribulation " to his eyes.[2]

There is a legend, which I am not myself inclined to believe, so completely out of keeping is it with his character, that, riding through the city and seeing a lady of whom he was enamoured enter a church, he spurred his horse and galloped in, through the great west doorway, to where she was kneeling. Another story, little better authenticated, though less intrinsically improbable, describes him as penetrating to the chamber of this lady, who, being happily married, had no desire for his attentions. Once there, he importuned her with his demands; but, instead of yielding to them, she uncovered her bosom and displayed a breast that was being slowly consumed by a loathsome cancer.

" See, Ramon," she cried, " the foulness of this body that has won thy affection ! How much better hadst thou done to have set thy love on Jesus Christ, of Whom thou mayest have a prize that is eternal ! "

This incident, if in fact it happened, must have been a shock to the ardent young man, but, by the summer evening on which he comes into this narrative, the volatility of his nature had reasserted itself and the lady who had so successfully repulsed him had been succeeded in his

[1] *R.L.*, p. 49, n. 4.   [2] *R.L.*, p. 17, n. 1.

affections by another. It was the composition of a song in
her honour that was the cause of his intense concentration.
The art of the troubadour, at that time, was in its heyday,
and Ramon, like many another well-educated young courtier, was an adept at it: some of his later verses, written in
the popular troubadour metres, suggest that the songs of his
wanton youth must have been as gay and elegant as any.

Never had he worked harder at setting words to an
elusive melody than now. "His whole understanding,"
records a Catalan biography of him written during his life-
time,[1] "was engaged and occupied in the composition of
this vain song." And then, as he sat there, alternately
warbling his air and scribbling his words, came the miracle
that changed his life.

For the hundredth time, perhaps, he looked up from his
writing and hummed another bar or two of the air, when
suddenly, as he gazed abstractedly into space, he saw that
Something was gazing at him. There, a little to his right,
against the wall, was " our Lord God Jesus Christ hanging
upon the Cross ".[2] It was no delusion of the imagination.
Nearly fifty years afterwards, the writer of the contemporary
biography describes the event as fully and vividly as though
it had happened only the day before. The expression of the
Crucified was one of "great agony and sorrow ".[3]

The effect which the vision produced upon the careless,
worldly young man was indescribable. He trembled with
fear. His pen fell from his grasp. He could neither think
nor reason. Forgetting what he had been doing, and thinking only how to escape from that sorrowing, piercing gaze,

[1] This, which was written in Catalan about 1311, will be referred to
in the text as the " contemporary biography " and in the notes as
C.B. I have published a translation of it, together with the corre-
sponding Latin text, as *A Life of Ramon Lull*, London, 1927. It is
remarkably vivid and detailed: a number of the fullest descriptions
in this book are drawn from it. [2] *C.B.*, p. 2. [3] *Ibid.*

" he threw himself forthwith upon the bed and lay down there ".

No doubt he went to sleep; and, when he rose on the next morning, decided that he must have been overwrought by his passion. So, on the next convenient evening, he sat down again in his room, with pen and paper, to resume work on his song. This time, hardly had he begun when, looking up, he saw the Crucified again. At this second appearance " he had much greater affright than at the first ",[1] and, pushing away his paper, flung himself upon the bed again, burying his face in his hands to shut out the terrible and persistent visitation.

But the unhurrying chase was not yet over; nor was it to end until its goal was won. Three times more, with a dogged determination that was to mark him throughout his life, Ramon took up his pen again to complete his song, and three times more there appeared that Figure, " in great agony and sorrow ", gazing at him with the same mute appeal. As the appearances continued, his shock lessened, and he began to reason. They were objective visions—of that he had no doubt. In that case, he asked himself, still fearfully, what could they mean? The " pricking of his conscience ", assisted perhaps by the Christian upbringing which he tells us he had received as a boy, supplied the only possible answer. " Our Lord God Jesus Christ desired none other thing than that he should wholly abandon the world and devote himself to His service."

One thought alone stood between him and the life which was soon to be his. Was he worthy? Could his sins be forgiven? Would one whose opportunities had been so great, yet whose past had been so utterly abandoned, be received into the company of Christ's servants? It was this obstacle, at first insuperable, which caused him such remorse

[1] *Ibid.*

as only great sinners and great penitents have known.   Then there was borne upon him " the great tenderness, patience and mercy which our Lord has toward sinners ".[1]   He took comfort.   And with comfort came the conviction that, " notwithstanding the life which until that day he had led, it was His will that he should devote himself wholly to His service ".[2]

The first step he took he describes to us, not in prose, but in his quaint monorhymed verse:

> Pardon I sought at break of day.
> Contrite and sad, I went straightway
> My sins before the priest to lay.[3]

The next step was to decide how he could best show his obedience to the heavenly vision.   He wanted to atone for his misspent years by making some great act of sacrifice. And, while he was meditating what this should be, there came into his mind some words from the Gospel which he must often have heard read : " Greater love hath no man than this, that a man lay down his life for his friends."   The sacrifice he would make must be himself.   He would become a missionary, and devote the whole of his life to preaching the Catholic Faith, until it should please God to grant him the crown of martyrdom.

That was not so easy a decision to make as it may sound, for before the taking of the vow came the counting of the cost—and Ramon Lull was not the man to omit that. We shall best understand him, in fact, if we realize from the first that he was a strange blend of extreme idealism and sound common sense: one can never be quite sure when to call him a practical man and when a visionary.   The ideal which he set up for himself at the time of his con-

[1] *Ibid*.   [2] *Ibid*.   [3] " Cant de Ramon."   Cf. *R.L.*, pp. 22-3.

version never left him: all through his life he was possessed by the belief that one day he would be martyred. But for the moment he was more concerned with the way in which this aim could be accomplished. He had determined to preach the Catholic Faith, but how could he? The education which had been given him was for the Court, not for the Church. As he "thought at great length upon this within himself", and no doubt compared his attainments with those of young clerics whom he knew, it seemed to him that beside them he was "illiterate": he "had learned naught, save only a little grammar".[1]

This, he thought, was a "great defect and weakness",[2] especially as he had the impulse, not only to preach, but to write—to write "books . . . against the errors of the unbelievers".[3] As he turned over his desires in his mind, there came to him alternate fits of despondency and confidence. He would have to learn not only "science", but Latin, Arabic, "and likewise the languages of all other unbelievers".[4] It would mean years of study—and he was no longer a boy. Yet the more he reflected upon the obstacles, the more convinced he was that God intended him to overcome them. For by himself he would never have thought of such an ambitious task: the idea must be of Divine inspiration.

Then further possibilities occurred to his fertile mind. If not a scholar, he was at least a successful courtier. He might perhaps be God's chosen vessel to bear Christian ideals before kings as well as Gentiles, and he would use in His service the favour which he could command in high places. He would still have influence, no doubt, with James the Conqueror; with his former pupil Prince James, now a grown man; with Prince Peter, who in time would succeed the Conqueror; perhaps with Alfonso the Wise,

[1] *C.B.*, p. 4.   [2] *Ibid*.   [3] *C.B.*, p. 5.   [4] *Ibid*.

King of Castile, who had married Peter's sister, Violante; and certainly with all kinds of people whom he had met at Court, or on his travels. So he would go abroad to the courts of Christian princes; he would importune prelates; he would even present his petitions to the Holy Father. He would beg them all to send out more missionaries, and, further, he would urge the foundation of missionary colleges for the teaching of " sciences " and the languages of the heathen. For the practical side of Lull's nature told him that these were an essential preliminary to foreign mission work if unbelievers were to be converted by argument and not merely overcome by a crusade of force.

These three resolves—to write books on apologetics, to work for the provision of missionary colleges and, finally, to lay down his life as a martyr—Ramon made immediately after his conversion. It may also have been as early as this that he evolved an idea which was later to occupy a leading place in his projects. This was the composition of a method (or, in medieval terminology, an " art ") whereby the truth of Christianity should be triumphantly and irrefutably established and the heathen should thus be confounded for ever.

These things decided, Ramon went to the nearest church, and " prostrate upon the ground, besought the suffering Christ with tears " to accept his self-dedication.[1] Then he returned home, to make preparations for the future, which occupied him for three months.

Towards the end of that period came what might be described as a " second conversion ". Summer had passed into autumn and the beginning of October brought the then newly instituted festival of St. Francis of Assisi. Ramon, as one would expect, attended Mass on that day,

[1] *C.B.*, p. 6.

and it chanced that the preacher laid great stress on the completeness of St. Francis' surrender. He had given up, not only his inheritance, but everything he possessed: even of his clothes he had stripped himself, that he might serve his lady Poverty with undivided love. The words went home to the conscience of the now impressionable young man. If he had been trying, during these months of preparation, to make terms with the world—if he had even been hoping to serve two masters—the preacher's message was sufficient to complete that conversion which the visions had begun. When he returned home from church, it was to make an act of complete renunciation. No more half measures! After setting aside a part of his possessions for the support of his wife and children, he sold the rest, and, distributing the proceeds among the poor, broke completely with his former life by leaving Majorca.

Crossing to the mainland, he went as a pilgrim to Santiago de Compostela—the city of St. James, Patron of Spain—in far-off Galicia, and to another shrine, which some have identified with Montserrat, near Barcelona, and some with Rocamadour, in the south of France. What else he did cannot be discovered. But when he returned, at the end of a year or more, it was to begin his studies. His first idea had been to go to the University of Paris; advisers whom he consulted, however, dissuaded him. Strengthened by his experiences at the sacred shrines, he must return to live as a Christian among those who had known him as a worldling, and thus witness to the genuineness of his conversion. For the rest, his ignorance being so great, he could learn as much as he needed in Palma—especially of Arabic, for, though it was now a Christian city, its population still included many Moors.

So, on his arrival, he at once cast aside " all superfluous clothing, such as he had been accustomed to wear, and

B

dressed himself in a habit that was very honest and of the
coarsest cloth he could find ".[1]   That must have given the
gay youths of Palma something to talk about—the ex-
royal-seneschal appearing in sackcloth!   And no doubt a
good many respectable and religious people looked askance
at him too.   For, after all, he was neither a cleric nor a
professed religious.   Though apparently he still lived in his
house, surrounded by his family, and his servants, he had
abandoned the primary duties of his married state and had
renounced his honourable calling for the fantastic pursuit
of an ideal.   He was now living nothing else but a life of
idleness!   Some thought him merely simple, and called
him a fool; others held him to be mad.   Social persecution
in the thirteenth century was less refined than now: the
people made no bones about deriding him in the streets;
his very servants gaped at him as they did his bidding.
But gradually he learned to live this down, and then, as he
himself tells us, to welcome it.

I am clothed with vile raiment, but love clothes my heart
with thoughts of delight.[2]

Ah, Lord God!   Thy servant thanks and blesses Thee for
that it has pleased Thee to give him greater fear of Thy judgment alone than of all the people who mock at him in the
streets—yet once he had greater fear of their judgment than
of Thine.[3]

Little is known of Ramon's studies in Palma, except
that they included Latin and Arabic.   From the high
standard which he reached in literary Arabic, one would
imagine that at this stage he was working at little else,
though later he must have read widely and deeply in
many other subjects.   At the first attack, he found Arabic
appalling—" like the voices and languages of beasts ",[4] as

[1] C.B., p. 8.   [2] B.L.B., 177.
[3] R.L., p. 38, n. 2.   [4] R.L., p. 40, n. 5.

he puts it in his downright way. To one who had probably no more than a smattering of any foreign tongue and little experience of the discipline of study, it would indeed be a formidable undertaking. Determined not to be beaten, he toiled at it for no less than nine years: by the time he felt proficient enough to enter upon his life-work, he was forty-two.

Only a single incident in the history of those nine years has come down to us, but that incident is at least a dramatic one. In order to progress the more rapidly, Lull had purchased a Moorish slave, who talked Arabic to him and apparently was sufficiently well educated to give him lessons too. One day, while he was out, the slave began to make blasphemous remarks about Christianity, and, when these were reported to Lull, he lost his temper and set about the Moor, striking him (says the contemporary biography) " on the mouth, the head, the face and on other parts of the body ".[1]

The Moor said nothing, but the incident rankled in his mind, for he had won a privileged position in the household by his skill as a teacher and he had never been treated in such a way before. As he brooded over the insult, he gradually determined upon revenge; and, one day, seeing his master sitting alone in a chair, he made for him with a knife.

" Now," he cried, " shalt thou perish! "

Taken completely by surprise, Lull could only parry the blow, and, before he had wrenched the weapon from his assailant, he had received a slight wound. The noise of the struggle brought the servants running to see what was the trouble: it was a simple matter to overpower the Moor and shut him up till his master should decide what to do with him.

[1] *C.B.*, p. 9.

In his unregenerate days, Ramon would not have
hesitated for a moment: they had a short way with slaves
in the Middle Ages. But now he was not so sure that he
would be doing right to kill him. It would be the safest
plan—for, if the miscreant were spared, who knew when
he might not bring out his knife again? On the other
hand, he felt so much in his debt for the years of help he
had given him that to put him to death seemed rank in-
gratitude. In his perplexity he went away for three days
to a Cistercian monastery not far from Palma to think over
the question further and to ask God's guidance. And in a
curious way the question was settled for him. When he
returned home, as perplexed as ever, he found, to his un-
speakable relief, that he no longer had the responsibility
of making a decision. For the Moor, evidently mis-
trustful of the quality of his master's mercy, had committed suicide by hanging himself with the cord which
bound him.

II

RANDA AND MIRAMAR

Memory and will set forth together, and climbed into the mountain of the Beloved.
—*B.L.B.*, 103

I T IS A STRIKING COMMENTARY on Ramon Lull's amazing energy that, during these nine years of study, he should not only have begun to write but should have written as much as most authors would be proud to have produced in a life-time. It would seem, however, that his first books grew quite naturally out of another activity which he probably found a relaxation after so much concentrated book-work. There were still a great many Jews and Moors in Majorca; and, although one may be sure they showed no disposition to risk expulsion by indulging in attempts to proselytize, Ramon conceived the idea of holding debates with them on religion. It was a happy thought, for he was able to carry out the plan with the approval, and under the patronage, of Prince James, who from time to time visited the island and kept in touch with him; the experience, too, was an excellent training for the debates which he would hold later in a hostile atmosphere and in heathen lands.

The exact date of the *Book of the Gentile and the three wise men*[1] is not known, but it was almost certainly written (in Catalan, like most of Lull's works) during the nine-

[1] *R.L.*, pp. 82-98.

year study period and probably at long intervals. It is the
earliest example of a type of work which he loved to write
—the religious allegory. A description of its framework
will illustrate its quite attractive conventionality. The
" Gentile " is a heathen philosopher, who " had no knowledge of God, neither believed in resurrection", and, to
beguile his sadness at the thought of death, decides to
travel. He encounters a typically allegorical forest, a place
of wondrous beauty, full of trees bearing the choicest
flowers and fruits and the home of birds and beasts of
great rarity. But the more beauty he finds, the greater is
his dismay at the inevitability of death and annihilation;
so he wanders about in the deepest distress.

Now, at about this time, three sages—a Jew, a Christian
and a Saracen—are travelling together from an unnamed
city. Resting by a spring, which waters five trees, they
discuss their respective beliefs, and sigh for a greater degree
of unity.

" Would to God," cries one of them, " that all men
might be led to embrace one law and one belief! That
there were no rancour or ill-will among them! That, even
as there is one God alone, all the nations might be united
into one, and for ever hold one faith, giving glory and
praise to our Lord God! "

The others echo his wish; and the three are about to
discuss their respective beliefs when they espy the Gentile:
" a great beard he had, and long hair, and he walked as
one that was weary and thin and pale, by reason of the
travail of his thoughts and his long journey." He, too,
halts by the spring, and, intrigued by " the strange appearance of the three wise men, and the strangeness of their
clothing ", gets into conversation with them and tells them
his troubles.

" How, fair friend! " exclaims one of the three. " Believest thou not, then, in God, neither hast hope of resurrection? "

" Alack, sir, nay," answered the Gentile, " and if ye can show me aught whereby my soul may have knowledge of resurrection, I pray you to do so."

So the sages resolve to prove to him " that God is, and that in Him are goodness, greatness, eternity, power, wisdom, love and perfection ". The exposition convinces him, and before long he is kneeling on the ground, with his hands and eyes raised to the heavens, thanking God that he has learned the truth.

Thus far, Lull's apologetics have been more picturesque than potent, for he has dealt with hardly any of a sceptic's real difficulties, merely setting before an imaginary sceptic considerations of an evidential nature and portraying him as capitulating unintelligently. As we shall see, Ramon was always too much inclined to make evil or untruth collapse on its initial contact with good, and the psychology of his romances suffers correspondingly. In this book, however, he may be forgiven for his departure from probability, since it is only after the Gentile's initial conversion that the main part of the argument begins. Once the first ecstasy of joy has passed, the unfortunate man remembers his parents and kinsfolk who have died in unbelief, and thus have presumably lost God's glory. Turning brusquely on his mentors, he asks them why they have no pity on those who have never heard of God and so cannot serve Him. How can they refrain from going out into distant lands as missionaries?

Then comes the crucial point of the narrative, for the sages' reply reveals to the Gentile that they have not one belief, but three. " And which of them," he asks in perplexity, " is true? " Whereupon " each of the three wise men made answer, praising his own belief, and attacking that of the others, and they had great strife together ".   •

The effect of their disagreement upon the Gentile can be imagined.

" Alas, sirs! " he cries. " Now have ye plunged me into sorrow and distress yet greater than those which I had aforetime! For then at least I had no fear of suffering, after my death, infinite torments. But now ye tell me that, if I walk not in the way of truth, there are tortures prepared for me to torment my soul after death eternally." In his despair he can only beg the wise men to argue their beliefs before him, and he will pray God to direct him to choose rightly which to adopt as his own. So the book settles down to be a " Book of reasons concerning the three laws "—by which title Lull refers to it elsewhere. Jew, Christian and Mohammedan now expound the principal tenets of their faith, and from time to time the Gentile breaks in and the exposition becomes a genuine discussion. Its most notable feature is an extreme fairness—one might almost say an excessive tolerance. The Jew, it is true, is by implication disposed of quickly, and the Christian not only describes his own beliefs but shows their superiority to those of his companions. All three cases, however, especially the Moor's, are presented with sympathy; the Christian is given the advantage neither of the initial attack nor of the final word, but has the weakest position of the three; and at the end of the book we are not told the Gentile's decision. He merely " washes his hands and face in the fair spring, by reason of the tears he has shed ", and announces that he will discuss the matter further with two fellow-heathen who are conveniently approaching.

It is a strange book—completely impersonal and completely devoid of fervour, eloquence and emotion. The sages, considering each believes that the others, unless con-

verted, will be damned eternally, display a quite inhuman
equanimity, taking leave of one another in " right friendly
and pleasant fashion" and each craving pardon " if he
had said any evil word concerning the laws of the rest ".
No doubt the author intended those sentiments to be
applied to himself. Fairness to his opponents was always
to characterize him, which no doubt was one reason why
he was so readily listened to. None the less, this early
work, picturesque though it is, lacks the drive and the conviction which we find in others. In manner and substance,
as well as in date, it belongs to his *juvenilia*.

When one surveys the other book written by Lull during
his nine years at Palma, it is easy to believe that the adventures of the Gentile and the sages were penned as a partial
relief from it. The *Book of Contemplation* is of enormous
size: in the modern Catalan edition, the text, without index
or commentary, occupies seven volumes, totalling nearly
three thousand large pages—say about a million words.
More remarkable still is the fact that it was originally
written—possibly with the help of the slave—in Arabic.
Even the translation of it into Catalan, with alterations
and improvements, occupied the author nearly twelve
months, and, as this seems to have been completed about
1272, or during his seventh year of study, his progress in
Arabic must have been extremely rapid.

Briefly (for any adequate summary of the work would
fill a fair-sized volume) the *Book of Contemplation* is
meant to be an " art ", or method, of " contemplation "
(that is, in his usage, " meditation ", " serious thought " or
" religious study "),[1] for daily use " by men learned and
men simple, secular and religious, rich and poor ".[2] It

[1] For a fuller elucidation of the word, see *R.L.*, pp. 62-3.
[2] *R.L.*, p. 54.

dwells successively on the attributes of God, on His works
of creation and redemption, on His ordinances as regards
man, on man's nature and on the Incarnation and Passion
of Christ. The latter part of the book consists of two
treatises, on love and on prayer—themes on which he was
later to write in a way that was to make him famous for
ever. The book has never been translated, as a whole,
into English; and, because it is not only so long, but has
been superseded in so many places by the later work of
Lull himself, it probably never will be. Parts of it, however, are of the greatest interest.

So frequent, first of all, are the reminiscences of the
author's own life that we may wonder if it does not in-
corporate parts of some diary which he kept from the time
of his conversion. The pictures of court life are detailed
and vivid to a degree. We see the king at his pleasures,
with his falcons, horses and dogs, with troubadours, singers
and musicians on the viol and lute, with *joglars*[1] and
" tellers of new things " to whom he gives money and
garments " that they may spread abroad his fame over all
the world ". The courtiers' garments are described, the
" spacious and painted halls " of their mansions, the
knights with their richly caparisoned steeds, the ladies,
painting their faces or embroidering their dresses and
taking care that no spot or stain shall defile them. Rich
banquets are set before us and " delicate wines " in goblets
of gold. When these are despatched and men rise from
table, there come *joglars* and flatterers with instruments of
music, singing songs and speaking of vanities.[2]

Nor are these Lull's only pictures of society. In the
third book there passes an immense procession of characters of every rank and occupation: rich prelates, who

---

[1] Minstrels, reciters of verse, and the like: the French *jongleurs* and
Spanish *juglares*.   [2] *R.L.*, pp. 46-7.

"give to the poor for the love of God in times of necessity";[1] monks and friars, devoted to prayer and mortification, and often subjected to cruel and unjust treatment; knights, "armed with wood and steel",[2] fortifying castles and consulting omens; pilgrims, with staff and scrip, some clad poorly, some "with sauces and barrels full of wine, with coin of gold and silver for their expenses";[3] judges and advocates, almost all corrupt, clad in sumptuous garments and riding on sleek palfreys; physicians, none too skilled in their trade and tainted with a similar love of luxury; merchants, with cloth, hides, beasts, jewels and what not; scriveners with parchment and ink; shoemakers cutting and sewing their leather; money-changers, craftsmen, furriers, weavers, butchers, barbers, millers, glaziers, potters, bakers, gardeners, taverners, couriers, criers, waggoners, municipal officers, gamesters, archers, calkers, porters, and a few more "offices" given only a passing mention: a notable assembly, both for its size and for the clearness with which, in a few bold strokes, each character is outlined.

The book has some striking references to love between a prince and his people, and among its significantly recurring figures is the faithful and admiring vassal. But on the whole it is the bad side of the medieval court, rather than the good side, which is shown us. Princes who should guard their people from injustice appoint procurators and judges who are open to corruption. Instead of ensuring their subjects' safety and improving the conditions under which they live, they are extravagant and wasteful and upon the slightest pretext plunge them into war. They maintain huge retinues and spend their days hunting while conscienceless officials prey upon the people. Nor are Lull's knights much better than his princes: given their

[1] *R.L.*, p. 57.   [2] *R.L.*, p. 58.   [3] *Ibid*.

rank that they may root out evil, they dishonour themselves by frequent quarrels and slay " just men and those
that love peace rather than war ".[1] More degraded still
has become the office of *joglar*; for, while their earliest
songs were in praise and honour of God, *joglars* sing
now only of lusts and vanities, and their ballads and
lays and music and dancing are held in the highest
esteem.

Right through the book there runs a strain of penitence.
Continually the author is recalling his past: " the estate
wherein I lived . . . companying with wild beasts and dead
in my sins; for my solace and pleasure were with men who
were beasts indeed."[2] He describes how, while his friends
and relatives trusted him, he did them nothing but harm,
but he also reiterates his resolve to do good and he reaches
out to the future as often as he looks back to the past.

> In the best time of my age, O Lord, I gave myself up wholly
> to sin . . . but now I would fain give up to Thee both myself
> and all things that are mine.[3]

Among the semi-autobiographical themes of the *Book
of Contemplation* one stands high above the rest: the conversion of unbelievers. This book alone establishes that
it was the ruling passion of his life. It offers—and
naturally, if our chronology is correct—close parallels with
the *Book of the Gentile* and it clearly reflects Lull's experiences of public debate. His criticisms of unbelievers in
general, for refusing to examine the religion in which they
have been born, and of Jews and Saracens in particular,
must frequently be paraphrases of onslaughts made *viva
voce*. But it is his eager, fervent pleas for evangelization
that give these pages at once distinction and appeal. Why

---

[1] *R.L.*, p. 48.   [2] *R.L.*, p. 49.   [3] *R.L.*, p. 50.

do not more Christians obey their Lord's last command?
" Since Thou, O Lord, art ever ready to aid . . . how can
any Christian fear to preach our holy faith to the infidels? "
" How can a Catholic fear to dispute with an unbeliever?
For as Thou didst cast out from Thy glory the error and
falsehood of devils . . . it is a light thing for Thee to con-
found the false opinions and the errors of unbelievers."
Timid Christians who hesitate to join battle with the enemy
have lost the perfect trust which they should have in God's
aid and power. They forget Christ and His precepts; they
are lacking in love for God and for their neighbour. The
infidels are at their very doors—sometimes they are their
own tenants—yet not so much as a protest is heard when
they blaspheme. Often, too, Christians hinder the conversion of Jews and Saracens by refusing to help and to
receive as their brothers those of them who are already
converted. " Many Jews would become Christians if they
had the wherewithal to live, and likewise many Saracens,
if the Christians did them not dishonour."[1]

Yet the conversion of the Moslem world is of the first
importance; for, on the one hand, if God will but break
the hard heart of the Saracen, he will find himself nearer
to Christianity than he has realized; and, on the other,
" once the Saracens were converted, it would be a light
thing to convert the rest of the world ". So it is the duty
of all, from " the Pope and the princes " downwards, to
send messengers to Moslems everywhere who shall argue
with them, " vigorously and valiantly ", even if the parishes
have to be short of priests in consequence. One must cry
more loudly, is Lull's argument, to those that are far off
(i.e., from God) than to those that are near. Were the
goodwill present, these things would soon be put into effect,
for the " letters and language " of the infidels would quickly

[1] R.L., p. 74.

be learned by those who now would preach in that language
if they knew it, and the courage and endurance of the
Christian missionary in face of violence and privation
would furnish a new argument for the superiority of his
religion over all others.

In these contentions we can already detect premonitions
of Ramon's own future activities; and, as now and then
his voice takes the note of passion, we sense an eloquence
that is to grow greater and graver as the years go on:

Ah, my Lord and my God! If it should be Thy pleasure
for Thy servant to go through streets and squares, to cities
and lonely houses, crying aloud Thy truth and the falseness
of the unrighteous, and fearing neither hunger nor thirst nor
death, then indeed would Thy servant have knowledge that
he would be remembered in the mercy of his Lord God.[1]

And now we return the last of these seven great volumes
to their shelves, to take up the threads of Ramon's life
in Palma. We left him, outside the cell in which his
murderous slave had been imprisoned, staggered at the
news of his suicide. He appears to have thought it un-
necessary to engage a successor. He may even have felt
that he had stayed too long in Palma, absorbed in his read-
ing and writing, when he might already have begun the
missionary work to which he had dedicated himself on his
conversion. We know from his own words how his im-
patience to be up and doing sometimes tormented him.
"Ah, Lord," he wrote when he had completed one-third
of his *magnum opus*.

So great desire has Thy servant to give Thee praise, that by
night and by day he toils and struggles as best he may to bring
to an end this *Book of Contemplation*; and then, when once it
is completed, he will go and shed both blood and tears for
love of Thee in the Holy Land wherein Thou didst shed Thy

[1] *R.L.*, p. 75.

precious blood. . . . Till this book be ended, Thy servant
and lover may not go to the land of the Saracens to give
praise to Thy glorious name. . . . Wherefore I pray Thee to
aid Thy servant . . . that he may speedily go and suffer
martyrdom for Thy love, if it be Thy will that he be found
worthy thereof.[1]

Now he has finished the *Book of Contemplation*, mastered
Arabic and gained a sufficient knowledge of " science " to
justify his embarking upon a life of evangelization. And
yet he seems in no hurry to start. Why not? What can
be holding him back?

The urge, I believe, to spend a long period in quiet
meditation. Probably he felt that the development of his
intellect had been starving the growth of his spirit. There
are signs in the *Book of Contemplation* that the desire for
a life of prayer has been struggling in him with the yearn-
ing for the life of a preacher.[2] Once he is free, he decides to
deepen his contemplative experiences before entering upon
the career of an active. So he leaves his house and his
books behind him, and goes up into a mountain to pray.

Seen from the entrance to Palma Bay, or from one of
the sunlit terraces of its western shore, the view of the twin
heights of Mount Randa is unforgettable. This huge
saddle-like mountain, breaking the long, level stretch of
low hills running to the south of the island, dominates both
the ridge of which it forms a part and the surrounding
plain. To many it may seem grey, stern and forbidding.
But to Ramon, who had gazed at it so often, it stood for
the security of silence and solitude : it was " the mountain
of the Beloved ".

By some more primitive track than the straight road
of to-day, and through country very different from the
almond-groves by which it is now fringed, Ramon crossed

[1] *R.L.*, pp. 101-2.　　　　[2] *R.L.*, p. 102.

the plain, to begin the ascent of the mountain. A steep stony path leads upward to the depression between the twin summits. Save for glimpses of the blue Mediterranean, the scenery is uninviting. Boulders strew the path; little grows anywhere, except shrubs and weeds. But the climber had no eyes for the things around him.

Pensively the Lover trod the paths of his Beloved. Now he stumbled and fell among the thorns; but they were to him as flowers, and as a bed of love.[1]

At last the heights were reached and the pilgrim found a cave which would give him shelter from the elements. What precisely his experiences were it is impossible with any certainty to say. The contemporary biography, confirmed by Lull himself,[2] tells us that at the end of a week, " as he was engaged in contemplation, with his eyes turned towards the heavens, there came to him in an instant a certain Divine illumination which gave him the form and order wherein to write the books that he had in mind against the errors of the infidels ".[3] That simple statement is decked out by other writers with a vast number of variations, from which the only deducible probability is that his experiences were both intellectual and spiritual. The former, however, must have predominated, for, on descending to civilization, Lull went straight to the monastery of La Real, two miles from Palma, and began writing again. Here he composed his famous *Ars Magna*, which, as he saw it, was the most fundamental of his treatises, professing, as it does, by means of a semi-mathematical " art ", to supply infallible answers to questions of theology, metaphysics and even natural science. By this means, not only were the faithful to be edified but the unbelievers were to be confounded once and for all.

[1] *B.L.B.*, 36.   [2] *R.L.*, pp. 105-6.   [3] *C.B.*, p. 12.

A science I have found that's new,
Whereby comes knowledge of the true,
And falsehood's followers grow few.
Infidels now their creeds will rue—
Tartar and Saracen and Jew—
For God therewith did me imbue.

After writing this book, which he had evidently worked out in his mind during his retreat, together, apparently, with several others, Ramon returned to Mount Randa for four months, " beseeching our Lord by day and by night that that *Art* which he had compiled might lead to His honour ".[1] His book, that is to say, having been written, he had now to decide how he could best expound it.

Descending to the plain, this time for good, Ramon found himself summoned by Prince James to visit him at Montpellier, where he habitually resided, as his father's " lieutenant " in the city and the surrounding barony. It was some years—perhaps six or seven—since James and Ramon had met in Majorca, and in the interval James had " heard it said " that Ramon had " written certain books "[2] which he was not unnaturally curious to see. No doubt the Prince's interest in Ramon's history, and the pleasure with which he had greeted him on his last visit to Majorca, had not been entirely untainted by disapproval. The best of men are apt to be suspicious of sudden conversions, and James, if no worse than royal personages of his day, was certainly no better. Had Ramon told him anything in Majorca about his projected treatise on Contemplation, which in 1268 he would hardly yet have begun to write? If we may judge from his character, with its combination of diffidence and common sense, he probably had not. In any case, all that he could have said would be of a vague and general nature, and the Prince might be forgiven if he

[1] *C.B.*, p. 13.   [2] *C.B.*, p. 14.

C

doubted whether the projects would come to fruition. But now all was different. Reports had reached Montpellier—having lost nothing, we may be sure, upon the journey—of Lull's supernatural experiences on Mount Randa, of the publication of an enormous and most learned work written in Catalan and in Arabic, and of the composition of an " Art " of some kind for the conversion of the heathen, which was said to be infallible. Beneath such rumours, even were they exaggerated, there must of necessity be an important basis of truth. Here was something definite for James to seize upon: he would see those books, and find out if their writer were really inspired or no.

So Ramon crossed the Mediterranean and made his way to a city which he would have known since boyhood and which he was often to visit again. Arrived there, he laid his works before his royal patron, who at once " caused the said books to be examined by a master in theology, who was a friar ·minor " and whose report was full of " great admiration and respect ".[1] The verdict encouraged Ramon to unfold to Prince James another of his projects and to solicit his practical help. He could not expect this help immediately; for, in the first place, James was pre-occupied by the preparations for his marriage to the sister of the Count of Foix, which took place in October 1275, and then, nine months later, James the Conqueror died, leaving his principal possessions—Catalonia, Valencia and Aragon—to his elder son, Peter, and Majorca, with Cerdagne, Roussillon and Montpellier, to James.

The plan which Ramon saw a chance of fulfilling was the establishment of a college for the training of missionaries in theology and languages. And such a college was actually founded by King James, at Miramar,

[1] *C.B.*, p. 14.

on the north-western slopes of Majorca, very shortly after his accession. Thirteen friars—a number symbolical of Christ and the Apostles—were to live in it, and to devote themselves especially to the study of Arabic, their maintenance being provided by a yearly sum, paid by the King, of five hundred florins of gold.[1]

This signal success appears to have raised Ramon's enthusiasm to fever-heat and marked the first great climax of joy in his life. Other successes were to be his, but none was to arouse in him the almost boyish ardour of this—the ardour of a traveller who has surmounted his first hill and caught the first intoxicating glimpse of new horizons. Miramar, he resolved, should be only the least of his many missionary foundations. Yet to him it would always be the dearest—not only, we may suppose, because it was to be the first of a great number, but because of the beauty of the scenery amid which it was set.

Even to-day one may visit its site and marvel at its loveliness. As its name denotes, it is in full view of the Mediterranean, lying in fertile country on the north-western slopes of the mountains. Wide sweeps of silver-grey olive groves set off the azure sea, and above the grounds which once belonged to the monastery dark overhanging pines lend grandeur to what without them might seem a too effeminate beauty. The contrast between the ascetic hermit, oppressed by unescapable responsibility and the unknown future, and the successful founder light-heartedly lauding his benefactor is not more striking than that between the austerity and bareness of Randa and the fair prospect of Miramar glimpsed from the grey wooded heights above it on a day when a sunset spreading gloriously over the ocean encourages the illusion that the scene is too wonderful to be real.

[1] *C.B.*, p. 15.

Ramon himself, who read in the book of Nature with as much avidity as in any other, can hardly have failed to dwell musingly upon this contrast. Away yonder, out of sight, lay Randa, austere as the life he had led there. Now for a time the world was to be pleasanter: instead of the parched lentiscus there was the lustrous evergreen oak; woods and running water took the place of slopes that were sullen and treeless; the isolation of the mountain top was succeeded by the companionship of gardens.

It is not hard to picture the busy yet restful life which Ramon led in these idyllic surroundings, though he seems to have stayed there for no long period, conceiving his predestined sphere to be a wider one than the little obscure monastery by the blue and silver sea. There is no record of his having taught in it: probably his work consisted mainly in supervision. He may well, for the most part, have lived the life of a contemplative, watching the development of the college, advising those who taught in it and inspiring both teachers and disciples with his own ideals.

Unhappily, like other of Ramon's initial successes, the Miramar foundation soon came to an end. For rather more than sixteen years we can trace its history: then, for what reason there is no means of knowing, or even of guessing, it was abandoned. All we know of its end is contained in one dramatic line from a poem written by Ramon in 1295, in which, pleading for more colleges like it, he exclaims parenthetically:

May he repent who brought that work to naught!

It was through the work of a single person, then, that the college was abandoned—and evidently Ramon believed the intentions of that person to have been evil.

Soon after the foundation of Miramar, Ramon made his first visit to Rome, to tell the Pope, who had authorized his project, of its realization, and to beg for the foundation of similar colleges "throughout the world".[1] He had chosen an unfortunate moment, however; his patron, John XXI, had just died, and a successor was not yet elected. It would clearly be some time before his representations could bear fruit, so for the moment he decided to engage in fresh activities.

How he spent the next five years of his life is not known. Probably in travel. It is generally believed that he went first to Germany, and tradition credits him also with visits to Abyssinia, Egypt, Palestine, Turkey, Greece, Morocco and the south of Spain. Two books, *Blanquerna* and *Felix*, which he wrote soon after his return, describe some of these countries in a way which suggests personal observation. From them, indeed, has been constructed a complete itinerary for his journeys.

In 1282, we pick up his tracks again in Perpignan, where he had another meeting with the Majorcan King. All had not gone smoothly with that mild and complaisant young monarch. His brother Peter, though charged by their dying father to respect James's inheritance, had given proof of his temperamental pugnacity by demanding that his brother should become his vassal. James had protested; but his territories were scattered, and his forces, like his character, were far weaker than Peter's. After nearly three years of bickering, he submitted, whereupon the assertive elder brother turned his attention to expansion in Africa, whence he was recalled by trouble in Sicily.

The terrible news of the massacre at Palermo, afterwards known as the Sicilian Vespers, would have reached Perpignan shortly before James and Ramon met there, but

[1] *C.B.*, pp. 15-16.

there is no evidence that they discussed it. Our sources, however, record quite a different kind of conversation, highly typical of the thirteenth century. In an atmosphere of massacres, dethronements, conquests, expeditions and struggles for power, the King of Majorca and his former seneschal sat down and discussed the sin of our first father! The King, it appears, was perplexed as to why Adam should ever have been permitted by God to sin, and why He does not do away both with sin and with punishment and bring all men to glory. Ramon hereupon offered to explain this, which he did in a hundred octosyllabic couplets of uninspiring verse called *The Sin of Adam*.

In 1283, Ramon passed from Perpignan to the neighbouring city of Montpellier, where he stayed for at least two years and settled down once more to write with great vigour. Most of the books he wrote are in Latin, based upon the *Ars Magna*, on which work he lectured in the monasteries and schools of the city. He appears also to have written a treatise on medicine, and it was certainly at Montpellier that he composed a handbook on religion for the use of his son Dominic, a youth just entering upon manhood. Events of some importance were happening in the world outside: the ambitious King Peter had been overtaken by death; his son Alfonso had invaded Majorca and dispossessed King James of that part of his inheritance. But Ramon, loyal Majorcan though he was, had other business to do than grieve for his former pupil and sovereign. On raced his pen over the paper at a speed so amazing that we can hardly credit it. And over and above all these Latin works, the treatise for his son, and a number of opuscules in Latin and Catalan too insignificant to mention, he found time to compose the book which many think his masterpiece—the famous religious romance known popularly by its abbreviated name of *Blanquerna*.

III

BLANQUERNA

" Say, O Fool! Wherefore hast thou so great love? " He answered: " Because long and perilous is the journey which I make in search of my Beloved, and I must seek Him bearing a great burden and yet journey with all speed. And none of these things can be accomplished without great love." —B.L.B., 212

I**T WOULD SEEM PROBABLE** that the greater part of *Blanquerna* had been written before Ramon Lull settled at Montpellier—perhaps, indeed, at Miramar, or, at latest, during the years' following the visit to Rome. But towards the end of the book we are told that it was written at Montpellier, so no doubt it was either revised or finished there. It would be natural, after all, if Ramon had begun the book on his travels, that his first task on settling down for a time should be to complete it.

The story, though long, is simple, and its outline may be sketched very quickly. Its hero, who gives it its name, is the son of devout and wealthy parents, Evast and Aloma, who " for much time and long " have lived together without children. He is brought up with great care, his parents' intention being to embrace the religious life once he is of age, and leave to him the management of their possessions. But, when they propose this to him, they find to their dismay that he has decided to lead the life of a hermit and wishes to take leave of them immediately.

Aloma, with a woman's quick wit, bethinks her of a friend's daughter, Natana, who may be able perhaps to dissuade him from his purpose and win his heart. But the only result of a carefully arranged interview between Blanquerna and Natana is that the girl becomes enamoured of the religious life and enters a convent, whither her mother, after a period of rebellion against the daughter's wishes, follows her. Blanquerna, too, takes a pathetic leave of his parents and departs, whereupon they decide to sell their estates (as Blanquerna's creator had done), endow a hospital, and appoint as its chaplain and administrator " a monk who was a priest, an old man, of good life and a native of other parts ". This done, they set themselves to wait upon the patients, and live from day to day by " begging for the love of God ".[1]

Meanwhile, Blanquerna has wandered into one of Lull's typical forests, " through the strangeness and solitariness of (which) place, and the heavens and the stars, his soul was highly exalted in the contemplation of God ".[2] A magical forest it is indeed, and a forest of allegory, for in it is " a fair palace right nobly builded ", inhabited by ten ancient men of venerable mien, who prove to be—a delightful conception!—none other than the Ten Commandments:

Blanquerna entered a great and beautiful hall wherein . . . were ten chairs of gold and ivory fairly carven, in the which sat the Ten Commandments in estate of great honour. Right nobly were they clad in silks and gold; great beards had they, and long hair; and in appearance they were as aged men. Each one held upon his knees a book, and wept and bewailed very bitterly.[3]

Blanquerna marvels at their grief, and, learning from

[1] Bl., p. 78.   [2] Bl., p. 155.   [3] Bl., p. 156.

Nor are the characters always drawn convincingly. The good ones, when they meet the bad ones, have an effect upon them which is altogether too instantaneous for the contact to seem in the least natural. Sir Narpan may for a time resist Blanquerna; Nastasia may put up a show of fight against her forbiddingly ascetic daughter; but the reader knows at once that they will eventually capitulate, and therefore has small interest in the struggle. Blanquerna, like Evast before him, goes through his unreal world, a Midas of morality, transforming all the bold, bad men he touches, and, by a painless and therefore fictitious process, making them as good as gold. Where any character proves recalcitrant to the treatment—the cellarer, for instance, the archdeacon and the chamberlain—he is punished by being left undeveloped and undefined, no personality at all, but a lay figure.

Yet such defects are few and of small importance by comparison with the book's abundant merits. That it can be translated, literally and in its entirety, into English, and read with delight, six and a half centuries after it was written, is sufficient commendation. As soon as we realize that it is a century older than Froissart, Chaucer and Wyclif, we see it in its true light—as a masterpiece, not only of Catalan literature, but of European.

First, it is by no means unsuccessful in characterization. Blanquerna, who fails to interest us as a youth, captivates us entirely once his adventures have begun. He is not above being tempted, and that sorely; and, in spite of the dizzy heights to which he rises, he retains his individuality. His progress from triumph to triumph is as regular and as rapid as that of any giant-killer of chivalry, but he has an inner sanctuary of the soul, which fleetingly, from time to time, we are allowed to see.

Even more skilfully and movingly presented than Blan-

querna is Aloma his mother—a woman of unusual strength
both of character and of affection, quick to see an advantage in debate, shrewd enough to consult her obstinate
husband only when her decision is already taken, eloquent
when love or grief moves her to words, and intensely
appealing when even her resource and persuasiveness are
reduced to impotence. Never does Ramon's art rise to
greater heights than in her laments to the Blessed Virgin
over Blanquerna's departure:

I have had but one son and he it is whom thy Son takes
from me. In peril of evil men and of wild beasts He makes
him to go; alone He will make him to be all the days of his
life; raw herbs he will eat; his clothing will be but his skin,
and his locks, and the air around him. Do thou look down
and see how fair is my son Blanquerna in his person and in
his mind: think thou how sun and wind and nakedness will
darken him and destroy the beauty of his features. When he
is cold, who will give him warmth? When he is sick, who
will tend him? When he hungers, who will give him to eat?
If he fears, who will strengthen him? If thou aidedst not my
son, even without my prayers, where would be thy pity and
thy mercy? Let the grief that I have for my son, as I behold
him going to his death, in affliction and penance, alone in the
forest, I know not whither, call to thy mind the grief that
thou hadst for thy Son when thou sawest Him done to death
and crucified.[1]

Other of Lull's successful characters are allegorical. The
Ten Commandments, for example, are considerably more
real than the shadowy monks and canons who move across
this ample stage. Faith and Truth, Understanding and
Devotion can all be clearly visualized; Sir Little-care-I and
Sir What-will-men-say, shown us only once, are instantly
recognizable when we meet them again some years later.
And there are a few other characters with the life and
warmth of human beings: the nameless bishop, for example,

[1] *Bl.*, p. 74.

who anticipates Blanquerna in resigning his see to devote himself to contemplation, and, of course, the Fool of Love, in which *rôle* Ramon here makes his first appearance:

There came into the Court a man with shaven head and clothed in the garb of a fool. In the one hand he carried a sparrowhawk, and in the other hand a cord to which was tied a dog which he led. This man greeted the Lord Pope and the Cardinals and all the Court on behalf of the Lord Emperor, and he spake these words: " I am Ramon the Fool, and I come to this Court by the commandment of the Emperor that I may exercise my profession and seek my companions." When he had spoken these words, he gave the sparrowhawk food, and afterwards made it come to his hand two or three times. After this he struck and beat the sparrowhawk with the cord to which his dog was tied, and again he cried to it that it should come to his hand; but the sparrowhawk, because the Fool had struck it and put it from him, escaped and flew out of the palace of the Pope, and became wild. When Ramon the Fool had lost his sparrowhawk, he struck the dog very severely two or three times; and, whensoever he called it, the dog returned willingly to him.[1]

Then the Pope asks Ramon who he is and why he has acted in this manner. " Lord! " he replies, " I desire to be a fool that I may give honour and glory to God, and I will have no art nor device in my words by reason of the greatness of my love."

The sparrowhawk signifies the men who assist not to sustain the honour and governance of thy Court without money or rewards; and when a man prays them and gives them naught they become disheartened, afflicted and slothful; wherefore they escape from among men and become wild. The dog signifies those men that are so greatly inflamed and kindled with love for the honour and the governance of the Court, to the end that God may therein be honoured, that, without satisfaction being given them by any man for the trials which they bear, they suffer these trials and anxieties

[1] *Bl.*, pp. 317-18.

by reason of men that desire to gain advancement in the Court, and they are pleasing to all men and agreeable.[1]

As skilful as the portrayal of the best of the characters in *Blanquerna* is the narration of the " examples ", anecdotes and fables with which the book is studded. Many of the vividly related episodes, it is true, which are alleged to have actually taken place, bear the most obvious signs of having been invented. The avowedly fictitious incidents, on the other hand, related by the characters are, as a rule, well presented. Most of them, directly or indirectly, are Oriental, and, as in some of his later books, Lull appears to have culled them himself from Arabic sources. The fables of the wolf's penance,[2] the parrot and the monkeys,[3] and the pine, the fig and the date[4] are cases in point. Each story is told clearly, with no waste of words, and equally brief and pointed is each moral. When the narration is at fault, it is generally through excess of brevity, though the contrast of this with the leisurely trend of the main story is rarely unwelcome.

Another notable characteristic of *Blanquerna* is the light which it throws on thirteenth-century society. Blanquerna's birthplace, though described only as " a certain city ", is clearly a city of Languedoc, and it is with the people of Montpellier and its environment that we mix in these pages. And I use the word " mix " deliberately. There is no longer a procession, a pageant of medieval types, as in the more imperfect art of the *Book of Contemplation*. Individual characters may be undeveloped, but the whole crowded stage, with its continually changing figures, is for ever alive with movement. The personages may be quaint,

---

[1] *Bl.*, pp. 318-19.   [2] *Bl.*, pp. 197-8.
[3] *Bl.*, p. 198 (Reproduced later in *B.B.*, pp. 80-1).
[4] *Bl.*, pp. 218-19.

unnatural, fantastic, but we accept them—and that is the
true test—as we accept the quaint and unnatural figures of
some modern fantasy. If they will not fit into our own
world, we are willing to go and live for a time in theirs.
The discerning mind can penetrate the unreality and extract
the truth.

Of the two opuscules which form part of *Blanquerna*,
by far the more striking is the *Book of the Lover and the
Beloved*. Complete in itself, this represents the climax, not
only of the romance but, according to present-day ideas,
of the whole of Lull's writing. Since Lullian studies have
taken renewed life and a more modern orientation, it has
come to be regarded as the centre-piece of his work, as the
book which points to the source of his inspiration and as
the earnest of his literary immortality.

In the oldest extant catalogue of Lullian writings—that
of 1311—the *Book of the Lover and the Beloved* appears
independently of *Blanquerna*, and the connection between
the two works is very slight. No characters or events of
the novel are alluded to in the *Book of the Lover and the
Beloved*, as they are in the *Art of Contemplation*; nor is
there any reference to it, direct or indirect, throughout. I
have very little doubt that the smaller work was written
before the larger and incorporated in it as an afterthought.
What happened may have been something like this. In
writing Chapter 98 of *Blanquerna*—that is to say, the last
chapter but two—Ramon has penned a very vivid and detailed description of a contemplative's idealized retreat,
based probably on his own experiences in Miramar and
Randa. By a natural transition, his thoughts turn to the
little book which he has himself made, probably for his
own devotional use, in such a retreat. He therefore in-
cludes it, by the easy device of representing it as the work
of Blanquerna, and makes it his ninety-ninth chapter. But

he has already written another opuscule—the *Art of Contemplation*—which he probably intended to be used in a
similar way: this he now adds as a final chapter. And
then, some kind of epilogue to the neglected and almost
forgotten narrative being necessary, one further addition
is made. The present hundredth chapter is written,
and the two opuscules are combined in one enormous
Chapter 99.

Two statements made in *Blanquerna* as to the origin of
the *Book of the Lover and the Beloved* may well have been
literally true. First, we are told that Moslem sources have
influenced its form. Blanquerna remembers a Saracen tell-
ing him of " certain men called Sufis " who " have words
of love and brief examples which give to men great devotion; and these are words which demand exposition, and
by the exposition thereof the understanding soars aloft,
and the will likewise soars, and is increased in devotion ".[1]
Secondly, the book is the outcome of actual contemplation. Blanquerna is asked by a hermit in Rome to write
him a manual of spiritual exercises; he agrees to do so,
but is unable to begin. So he resolves to " give himself
fervently to the adoration and contemplation of God, to
the end that in prayer God should show him the manner
wherein he should make the book and likewise the matter
of it ". And, while he is " carried away in spirit ", it
" comes to his will " that his book should be rather different
from what he had intended.[2] Then follows this description
of how it was composed:

Blanquerna was in prayer, and considered the manner
wherein to contemplate God and His virtues, and when he
had ended his prayer he wrote down the manner wherein he
had contemplated God: and this he did daily, and brought
new arguments to his prayer, to the end that after many and

[1] *Bl.*, p. 410.   [2] *Bl.*, pp. 409-10.

divers manners he should compose the *Book of the Lover and the Beloved*, and that these manners should be brief, and that in a short space of time the soul should learn to reflect in many ways. And with the blessing of God Blanquerna began the book, the which book he divided into as many verses as there are days in the year, and each verse suffices for the contemplation of God in one day, according to the art of the *Book of Contemplation*.[1]

Three *dramatis personæ* (if the phrase be allowable) appear in the book: the Beloved, the Lover and Love.

The Beloved is God—the God of Christianity, Three in One, One in Three—immanent and transcendent, Creator and Redeemer of mankind: above all, a God of love, Who can be sought and found by man, through beauty, through goodness and through truth:[2]

" O Beloved," said the Lover, " I come to Thee, and I walk in Thee, for Thou dost call me."[3]

" Thou, O my Beloved, art so great a Whole that Thou canst abound, and be wholly of each one who gives himself to Thee."[4]

More particularly, the Beloved is represented as the Lord Jesus Christ, considered as the Redeemer and the Sacrifice for our sin and the supreme Object of our love.[5] There is no dwelling on physical aspects of the Passion: the Cross is spoken of as a " Place "[6] and the shedding of blood is idealized into the wearing of crimson garments,[7] just as the act of Incarnation is described as Christ's coming " in the vesture of His Lover ".[8] In Himself, and in Christ Jesus, God the Beloved Father loves man with an " infinite and eternal love, perfect and complete ".[9] All who love Him He makes to abound in love, arming them for their battles, rescuing them in peril, tending them in sickness, healing

[1] *Bl.*, p. 411.   [2] *R.L.*, p. 181, nn. 2, 4-7.   [3] *B.L.B.*, 297.
[4] *B.L.B.*, 68.   [5] *B.L.B.*, 101, 153, 276, 313, 135.   [6] *B.L.B.*, 67.
[7] *B.L.B.*, 262. Cf. 91.   [8] *B.L.B.*, 30.   [9] *B.L.B.*, 111.

D

their wounds, but grieving not for the grief and the trials
which come to them with the healing, for these are His gifts
and they but bring them nearer Him.[1]

Tormented was I by love, O Beloved, until I cried that
Thou wert present in my torments; and then did love ease my
griefs, and Thou as a guerdon didst increase my love, and love
doubled my torments.[2]

The Lover is " a faithful and devout Christian ",[3] called
by God to a life of self-denial and devotion, seeking his
Beloved by paths that are perilous and long, wearying his
body, casting away his wealth and leaving the joys of this
world. He is completely weaned from temporal delights,
his joy being to serve God, and his grief to see men neglect
and offend Him. He desires to live, while his Beloved
wills, so that he may serve Him upon earth; when he dies,
he desires to die as a martyr.[4]

Between these two clearly outlined figures comes a somewhat vaguely defined third—the allegorical figure of Love.
For the most part, Love is the Lover's close companion.
When the Lover is in rapture, Love swoons; when he for-
gets the Beloved, Love falls sick, or vanishes and cannot be
found; when he sleeps, Love dies, but revives when he
awakens.[5]   Elsewhere, Love becomes a more transcendent
personality, dowering the Lover with noble gifts, or with
grievous trials, imprisoning him—body, mind and soul—
yet " nurturing and directing " his life, so that at his death
he may be able to vanquish his enemies.[6]   And always he
is an essential element in the communication of Lover with
Beloved: the Lover " cannot reach the Beloved unless he
pass through Love ".[7]

[1] *B.L.B.*, 3, 6, 214, 133, 303, 23, 244, 31, 230.   [2] *B.L.B.*, 109.
[3] *Bl.*, p. 410.   [4] *R.L.*, p. 182, nn. 16-20, p. 183, nn. 1-2.
[5] *B.L.B.*, 89, 208, 210, 240.   [6] *B.L.B.*, 110, 223, 113, 114, 168, 207.
[7] *B.L.B.*, 258, 259.

world have different meanings for the Lover and for the worldling. What, to the Lover, is happiness? " It is sorrow borne for Love." What is loneliness? It is the companionship of many people. What is dishonour? It is forgetting the Beloved. Who is rich? " He that loves truth." To the Lover there is no distinction, such as the world makes, between joy and sorrow, pleasure and pain. Fear is unknown, for so long as his heart is fixed upon God. Night, which men use for sleep, is given him for meditation. Solitude, which men shun, means for him the truest companionship. Death, which men dread, is to him but one of the gates to the Beloved's city.[1] All these things, and many more which the book expounds, are to the world foolishness, and they are gathered up into one pregnant paragraph which describes first the outward manifestation, and then the sublime viewpoint, of the hidden life:

" Say, O Fool! What meanest thou by a marvel? " He answered: " It is a marvel to love things absent more than things present; and to love things visible and things corruptible more than things invisible and incorruptible."[2]

On the poetry of the *Book of the Lover and the Beloved* there is no need to dwell, so completely does it expound itself to every reader. Here, as in other respects, Lull's powers were at their height when he wrote this book. The vividness of his parables—often of only four or five lines— is not more remarkable than the simplicity of the devotional passages which kindle with poetry as well as with love. At their best, these paragraphs are unforgettable.

Nowhere in all his work is Lull more sensitive than here to the wonders of Nature. While he produced nothing as sublime, or as sustained in its sublimity, as St. Francis' great " triumph song of oneness ", he is yet so conscious

---

[1] *B.L.B.*, 65, 86, 47, 108, 196, 119, 121, 147, 46, 47, 342; *Bl.*, p. 532.
[2] *B.L.B.*, 84.

of the Divine immanence in Nature that at times he seems
to be writing a poetical commentary on this very theme.
He is in the direct line of those mystics who have found
their Creator at once in the shining of the stars, in the
flowering of His fields, and in His ways with men. So we
can watch with him the turbulent stream, the majesty of
the lightning, the swift gathering of the waves of the sea,
the sunlit clouds shining as brightly as the daystar or the
moon, the eclipse in the heavens which brings darkness over
all the earth. We are warmed by the splendour of the sun;
we watch it go down and withdraw its brightness; we walk
in gardens or fruitful orchards, drink of their cool, clear
springs, and rest in their grateful shade. We hear the singing of the birds at dawn in garden and forest, but we hear
them also as we tramp over hill, valley and plain, along
rough and thorny paths, both long and short, climbing
up into the mountain (expressive phrase!) and, from the
heights, descending not only to the plains but to the depths
of precipices. Not sight alone, but every sense we possess,
is evoked by this nature-lover and poet. We listen to the
breeze stirring the faintly trembling leaves; we catch the
faintly borne perfume of flowers.[1] And whither does this
sensitiveness, this keen delight in the visible world, lead us?
Always to one point—to the Divine Nature.

During the centuries which have intervened between
Lull's day and our own, a misguided enthusiasm for exposition has led to many unfortunate attempts being made
to " explain " Lull's masterpiece to the simple, attempts
both fantastic and prosaic, which too often have explained
away the poetry of the book as well as its devotion. Fortunately, in these modern days, critics have recovered a
text which must be as nearly as possible the primitive text
of Lull and editors have been content to present it without

[1] *R.L.*, p. 189, n. 4, p. 190, nn. 1-18.

commentary, so that it may give its own message.   And in this message, as we shall presently show, lies the most characteristic quality of the Lullism of the twentieth century.

IV

FIRST AFRICAN MISSION

*The Beloved said to His Lover: " Thou shalt
praise and defend Me in those places where
men most fear to praise Me." The Lover
answered: " Provide me then with love."*

—B.L.B., 135

IN MARCH 1285 Ramon turned Romewards once more,
and this time his visit was attended with greater success
than it had ever been in the past. Its beginnings were not
auspicious, for no sooner had he arrived at Rome than the
mischance of eight years earlier was repeated: the news
reached him that Martin IV, another of the French popes
who might have favoured his plans, had just died at
Perugia. Martin's successor, however, Honorius IV, was
elected almost immediately, and in him Ramon found one
who believed both in his plans and in his ability to translate them into action—one who, further, was himself a man
of action. Advised and encouraged by Lull, he set up a
school of Arabic and other languages of heathen peoples
in no less important a centre than Paris; and it is even said
that he established one in Rome.

Delighted at the acceptance of his plan, Ramon stayed
in Rome for a year, adding at least two items to his
bibliography. One of these was a verse-book—*The
Hundred Names of God.* In the Korân, remarks the
preface, " the Saracens say that there are ninety and nine
names of God, and that he who knows the hundredth Name

will know all things. Wherefore I make this book of the Hundred Names of God; and, since it follows not that I know all things, I do it to reprove their false opinion." The second work was in Latin: *The Book of the Tartar and the Christian*, which re-introduces the hermit Blanquerna and expounds the *Quicunque vult*. Having finished these, Lull went to Paris, armed with letters from Honorius, which recommended that he should be allowed to expound both his projects and his doctrines in the University.

The Chancellor of the University of Paris during part, if not the whole, of Ramon's stay there was the somewhat notorious Berthauld de St. Denis, whose dictatorial and autocratic rule involved the University in such continual tumult that he had in the end to be sent to Rheims as Archdeacon, whence he was promoted shortly afterwards to the bishopric of Orleans. A fine, if vehement orator, and a learned and intrepid theologian, Berthauld was nevertheless unfitted to govern a university at a time when theological feeling ran so high. It may have been[1] on this account that Ramon's stay in Paris was not a long one. Forty experts, says tradition, were instructed by the Chancellor to examine the *Ars Magna*, and they all concurred in sealing it with their approval, with the result that Ramon was given the title of " Master ", which from that time forward he uses to describe himself in his own writings. None the less, there is a sentence in the contemporary biography into which a good deal can be read:

And when he had been there for some time and had seen the manner of the University he went to Montpellier.[2]

In Paris, as in Rome, and, it would seem, everywhere

---

[1] Cf. *R.L.*, pp. 201-2, for the chronology of this period, which is somewhat confused. In this narrative I follow the contemporary biography. [2] *C.B.*, p. 17: cf. pp. 16, 58.

else, the indefatigable apostle wrote feverishly. Only one of the books which he produced there, however, is of any consequence—a companion romance to *Blanquerna* entitled *Felix, or the Book of Marvels*. The hero of this is a boy sent by his father on a journey round the world to view its wonders. His opening adventures are typical. A shepherdess whom he meets in a forest believes that God will protect her from harm, but is killed by a wolf; whereupon he begins to doubt God's providence. A hermit, however, by demonstration, anecdote and object-lesson, restores his faith, and afterwards, at his request, instructs him as to the nature of the Godhead, the Unity of God, the Holy Trinity and the Creation, pointing out, in so doing, the importance of exercising the understanding as well as of having faith. At the conclusion of this instruction, which is enlivened by occasional dialogue, Felix leaves the hermit and continues his travels, meeting with a woman in great sorrow who is going to seek consolation of Blanquerna. They discover him beneath the usual " fair tree " with " a book wherein was much learning of theology and philosophy wherewith he contemplated the King of Glory ". Needless to say, he is able at once to console the woman, who thereupon disappears from the story, leaving Felix sitting at Blanquerna's feet and being instructed upon the Incarnation, the Passion, original sin, the Blessed Virgin, the prophets and the apostles. This scene ends Book I.[1]

The remaining books, on Angels, Elements, Heavens, Plants, Metals, Beasts, Man, Paradise, Hell, are of much the same type, with their didacticism lightened by occasional vivid episodes. One of these occurs when Felix encounters Sir Little-care-I and Sir What-will-men-say, who are engaged in a violent dispute on the nature of true honour.

[1] *R.L.*, pp. 207-8.

Walking along together, they come to the gate of a city, whereupon Sir What-will-men-say insists upon donning the crimson hose and elegant shoes that he has brought with him, and even upon changing his garments, lest any should fail to take notice of him. His companions reply that, since nobody knows them, it matters little if they go unshod, and they refuse to wait for him. "Proudly and with great ostentation" he walks alone through the main street of the city, but the only attention he receives is from two merry youths, who mock him and endeavour to pull off his fine garments. Enraged, he draws his knife upon them; a quarrel ensues, and both he and one of the youths are slain. One of the most promising characters in the book having thus been disposed of, Felix and Little-care-I continue their journey in a much sobered mood, and meet with various adventures. Before long, however, a new hermit comes upon the scene and Felix begins his lessons once more.[1]

The conclusion of the book is not quite conventional. Considering himself at last " well instructed ", Felix leaves the hermit and travels on till he reaches an abbey where he offers to stay for a time and relate the marvels he has seen. So delighted are the monks that they insist upon his taking their habit and continuing his way as a member of their Order. But, before he can start, he falls ill and dies; the author had apparently forgotten that he had made Felix' father compile the book *Of Marvels* on his son's return from his travels![2]

Though by no means devoid of interest, *Felix* falls a long way in merit below *Blanquerna*. With few exceptions, the characters are merely pegs on which to hang instructions: even Felix, and, in this book, even Blanquerna, are only lay figures. So soon as a character is no longer needed,

---

[1] *R.L.*, pp. 210-11.   [2] *R.L.*, pp. 213-14.

he disappears from the tale and the author does not even trouble to tell us why.

There is no plot-interest in the story: one might almost say there is no story. The hero provides only a superficial unity. No reader cares where Felix goes next or what hermit he meets—for they are all " prudent, wise and learned ". The improving anecdotes, for the most part intolerably artificial, are bandied to and fro like tennis-balls. In short, the book shows a surprising loss of power. One would think it the work of an old man—yet only a year or two had passed since Lull had finished *Blanquerna*.

One part of *Felix*, however, which has been translated into English, far surpasses the rest: the section—in reality an independent opuscule—entitled *The Book of the Beasts*. In it Lull uses a collection of animal tales, belonging to the " Reynard the Fox " cycle and derived from Oriental sources, called *Kalila and Dimna*, but he transforms so much of the borrowed material that it may in every way be considered his own. The original is verbose, involved and sententious; Lull's narrative, on the other hand, is well constructed, full of incident, never halting for long and propounding real problems in the solution of which we take a genuine interest. Throughout the narrative we are kept amused by the shrewdness with which Dame Reynard sub-stitutes small and timid beasts in the king's privy council for large and strong ones. The finest part of the story is the lion's intrigue with the leopard's mate during her lord's absence and the subsequent murder of the aggrieved party. The interview between leopard and weasel strikes a deep note of genuine pathos; and the narrative of the battle be-tween the leopard and the ounce gives us a climax that, in a story about human beings, would be one of tense excite-ment.[1] Only less interesting because less original is the

[1] *B.B.*, pp. 61-2, 66-7.

description of the ox's disillusionment in the service of man and his subsequent victimization by Dame Reynard.

A beast story so strictly conventionalized offers little scope for characterization, but in the lion, the fox and the leopard Ramon has made the most of his opportunities. Perhaps the most pathetic pair are two of the little people of the lion, the rabbit and the peacock, who, having sworn a forced oath to the fox and the elephant that they will keep their guilty secret, are frightened by a more imposing display of force into betraying it. It is surely a hard heart that does not wish them back again in the royal favour—unless, indeed, they are more secure outside it:

But when Dame Reynard had made an end of speaking, the king looked at the rabbit and the peacock after a manner that was most terrible, and uttered a great roar, to the end that in the consciences of the rabbit and the peacock the nature of his high office might have greater virtue than the fear which they had of Dame Reynard. And when the lion had uttered a great roar, he commanded the rabbit and the peacock, with great wrath, to tell him the truth; and they could no longer restrain themselves, but told him all the truth. Then the king, with his own hand, slew Dame Reynard, after the which thing his court returned to its former good estate, and the king made the elephant and the bear and other honoured barons to be of his council, and cast out therefrom the rabbit and the peacock.[1]

Further points of interest in the *Book of the Beasts* deserve brief mention. The quaintness with which animals relate anecdotes of men and women, as in stories of human beings men and women do of animals, it has in common with other works of its nature. It goes farther than some of these in making its personages, especially the wily Dame Reynard, talk religion and cite Scripture for their purpose. On one occasion, and perhaps on two, it refers to its author: in the story of the Christian with the " Saracen slave in

[1] *B.B.*, pp. 89-90.

whom he greatly trusted ", but who " had no goodwill towards him, and considered daily how he might slay him ",[1] and in the picture of " a man poorly clothed, and having a long beard ", reproving the king of men in his own banqueting-hall[2] in the same way as Ramon the Fool had no doubt done more than once and was to do yet again. Both in portrait and in legend the Ramon of 1286 is depicted as having a *barba florida*, and he generally depicts himself thus from now onward.

At Montpellier, where in 1289 a number of existing schools were formed into a university, Ramon lectured on his *Art* as he had done in Paris, and continued to write books in amplification of it. Twice at least between 1287 and 1291 he visited Rome; and he remained in constant touch with the Holy See on the question of missionary enterprise. In the latter year, however, he experienced one of the severest crises of his life, described for us by the contemporary biography in the greatest detail. For the first time (so far as is known) he had planned to go himself to a Mohammedan country and preach the Gospel. Acting, perhaps, on a sudden impulse, he travelled to Genoa, intending to go by sea thence to North Africa. But, just as he had assembled his luggage and taken his passage on the boat, there came to him " a mighty temptation ". The enthusiast who, at the time of his conversion, had so joyously looked forward to making the supreme sacrifice, now began to count the cost of his perilous adventure. " His understanding showed him, as clearly as if he saw it, how that, so soon as he reached Barbary, the Moors would neither hear him, nor permit him to dispute or to preach, but would stone him, or at the least condemn him to perpetual imprisonment."[3] This conclusion, for the

[1] *B.B.*, pp. 13-14.   [2] *B.B.*, p. 51.   [3] *C.B.*, p. 18.

moment, seemed to him inescapable. He had better not go. And, suiting the action to the decision, he disembarked and allowed the boat to sail without him.

But no sooner had it left than the irresolute apostle found himself in the grip of a reaction. What had he done? He had faltered before the prospect of danger. He had committed a sin for which God would surely send him to hell. Worse still, his cowardice would become known and people who had looked up to him would lose their faith in God's power. So grievously did his remorse torment him that he fell ill. The nature of his illness no doctor could discover, nor would he himself reveal it; but the biographer goes so far as to say that he was "near to death".[1]

Yet while he lay there—still, of course, in Genoa—he heard someone say that there was a galley in the harbour preparing for a journey to Tunis. His heart leaped at the news: here was an opportunity for him to retrieve his honour! Ill though he still was, he determined to sail in it, and he would have done so but for a blank refusal from those in whose charge he was to carry him down to the harbour. But, now that he had battled with himself and conquered, his health began to improve; and when, a few days later, he heard of another Tunis-bound boat, he prevailed upon his friends to let him go, and, once on board, urged the sailors to put to sea lest anything else should impede his departure.[2]

No sooner was he afloat than his mysterious malady left him, giving place to an overwhelming joy. By the time the boat reached Tunis he was as well as he had been in his life, and, disembarking, he threw himself into his self-imposed work with a boyish eagerness.

A detailed account of his methods is given by the con-

[1] C.B., p. 21.   [2] C.B., p. 23.

temporary biography. Far from merely preaching to all and sundry, he spent some days in " seeking out those that were most learned in the sect of Mahomet, declaring to them how that he had studied the law of the Christians, whose faith and its foundations he knew well; and now had come there to learn of their sect and belief; and if it were found that this was better than that of the Christians, and they could prove it to him, he would assuredly become a Moor ". The challenge was taken up by " all the learned Moors " of the city, and (according to the biography) Ramon would answer them so well that they were " all astonished and confounded "; whereupon he followed up his advantage by preaching a sermon, part of which the biographer reproduces.[1]

The success of this kind of debate seems to have been sufficient to cause the preacher to be arrested and denounced to the Caliph, who, on the advice of a majority of his council, sentenced him to death. A powerful member of the council appealed in his favour and the sentence was changed to one of banishment. As soon as its commutation became known, a band of Moors— whether these were friendly or hostile to him is not clear —dragged him from his cell towards a Genoese boat which was lying in the harbour and about to sail. But, during the deliberations of the council, public feeling in the city had been stirred against the foreigner. When he appeared in the streets, showers of stones and a storm of blows fell about him, and probably only the protection of those who were haling him to the boat saved him from being stoned to death then and there.[2]

It might be supposed that Ramon was relieved, if not overjoyed, at his narrow escape from the mob. But he was no longer the man of little faith that he had been at Genoa.

[1] C.B., pp. 24-6.   [2] C.B., pp. 26-7.

All that he could think of, as he was being dragged along the streets to the harbour, " in peril of death, reviled, cursed and plucked by the beard ",[1] with fierce, swarthy faces all around him, was the loss of opportunities which would be entailed by his departure from Tunis. What of these souls, brought by his teaching, through the grace of God, to the point of preparedness for baptism, if he left them to sink once more into their former ignorance? To remain would be to die, yet his departure would be for them death eternal.[2]

The choice was an easier one for him to make than that which had faced him during his mental agony in Genoa, and we may be sure that he had not a moment's hesitation. Deposited by his captors in the ship, he waited till they had gone and the tumult had subsided; then slipped away, returned to the land, and found a retreat where he could lie in safety until the opportunity came to re-enter the city and resume his preaching. As he lay there, however, an incident took place which showed him the hopelessness of his plan. Some Christian—a merchant, no doubt—was going about the city of Tunis on his business. Unfortunately for him, he resembled the preacher in clothing and gesture, and no sooner did the people catch sight of him than they rushed upon him and would have haled him off and stoned him incontinently had he not had the wit to cry out at the top of his voice: " I am not Master Ramon." The real Ramon was wise enough to take warning from this event of the inflammable state of the Moors in the city just then. Without more ado, he crept back to his ship, not abandoning by any means the mission which he had hoped to continue in Tunis, but postponing it to a more convenient season.[3]

Never inactive, Master Ramon was no sooner at sea

[1] *R.L.*, p. 244.　　　　[2] *C.B.*, pp. 27-8.　　　　[3] *C.B.*, p. 28.

again than he began a new book, which he finished at Naples, whither the boat took him, four months later. Here, too, he lectured on his *Art*, and wrote a number of other books, one of which, the *Book of the Five Wise Men*, resembles the earlier story of the three sages and the Gentile. But, while he was still writing, there came to Naples the astounding news of the election to the Papacy of Celestine V. After an interregnum of over two years the Cardinals had conceived the extraordinary idea of electing a frail and emaciated hermit, seventy-nine years old, of visiting his retreat in the mountains, and, overruling his pleas of incompetence, of leading him through tens of thousands to his coronation. It was not to be supposed that the reign of such a pope could be anything but short and turbulent. From first to last he was the helpless tool of younger and more ambitious men, both clerical and lay. When at length, from sheer inanition, he laid down his sacred office, and exchanged supreme power for cruel confinement, it was to die after a few short years, to be canonized in 1313 by the Church and to be made notorious by Dante as an example of moral weakness,

colui
che fece per viltate il gran rifiuto.[1]

It is not clear why Ramon Lull should have hoped for anything from this hermit-Pope. True, Celestine was own brother to Blanquerna—a contemplative, yet called, as Blanquerna had been, to an active life in the service of the Church; a devout and holy man, beloved of the extreme party of the time known as the Spirituals, and in principle likely enough to sympathize with Ramon the Fool. Yet he should have known by this time that sympathy alone would gain him little. None the less, he went straight to

[1] *Inferno*, III, 58.

the Papal court, with a document (still extant) entitled
Petition for the conversion of the heathen.

In this he expounds his various projects with a fullness
which we have not previously encountered. Let a tithe of
the Church's entire wealth be assigned to crusades and
missionary work till the Holy Land is conquered and the
world won for Christ. Let one Cardinal be chosen to spend
his life searching for the best preachers " in all countries of
Christendom "—" holy men, religious and secular alike,
who to honour our Lord God would fain suffer death ".
Let these preachers be taught, among them, all the
languages of the world. Let colleges for the learning of
foreign tongues be founded in Tartary as well as in
Christendom. Let schismatics be recalled to the one fold,
for it is they—no doubt the Eastern sects are referred to—
who can best convert Moslems and Tartars.

How dreadful it will be, continues the *Petition,* if the
entire Mongol world embraces the religion of Saracen or
Jew. At present it is not difficult, by means of disputations, to convert them, for the religion they have is rudi-
mentary and they allow our missionaries free access. But,
if the Tartars set up a religion, as Mahomet did, all
Christendom will be in dire peril.

" I would fain say more," ends the *Petition,* " but I fear
lest I have said too much. If indeed I have been pre-
sumptuous, I crave forgiveness. But most of all I beg that
I myself, unworthy as I am, may be sent to convert the
Saracens, that I may do honour among them to our Lord
and God."[1]

It is to be supposed that the presentation of these
writings had but little effect on the worn-out hermit-Pope,
who, after a reign of five months, laid down his heavy
burden, to be succeeded by the able and ambitious

[1] *R.L.,* pp. 252-4.

Boniface VIII, a politically-minded pontiff upon whom Ramon had no influence at all. Recasting his petition, he had a number of audiences with him, all of which ended in failure. In the corrupt and intriguing Papal court, indeed, his persistence and devotion only made him enemies.

Of his reactions to these rebuffs he has left an eloquent record in a long poem written in the year of Boniface's election—perhaps the best piece of work in verse that he ever composed: the *Desconort* (" Disconsolate "). Its pathetic sub-title explains that it was "made by Master Ramon Lull in his old age, when he saw that neither the Pope nor the other lords of the world would put forth a method for the conversion of the heathen, according as he had prayed them at many and divers seasons ".

The poem is not an easy one to translate, for each of its sixty-nine twelve-lined stanzas has only a single rhyme, but a few extracts, as well as conveying its main drift, will give something of its flavour. It first relates the story, which we have already traced, of Lull's early life, conversion and thirty years of struggle for the adoption and translation into action of his ideals. Disconsolate at his many failures, he goes into a wood to be alone. There he sees a venerable hermit, with a long beard, a staff in his hand, and little clothing on his back beyond a hair-shirt. "Why art thou so sorrowful? " asks the hermit. Ramon tells him, and meets with long-desired sympathy. Had he but some success to report, he would reckon no trials that he had suffered excessive. But even his comrades laugh at him.

> Lonely am I, abandoned and unsought.
> I look men in the face—would tell my thought—
> But few are they that heed: the rest say naught,
> Then call me fool.

All to whom God has given most honour on earth despise him and his words, as though they were the words of one who " foolishly speaks and nothing does at all ". His *Ars Magna*, given him by inspiration from Heaven, which can impart knowledge of " all natural things ", he holds for lost: " scarce any for it cares." He can never know joy again.

The hermit endeavours to console him. If Ramon has done his utmost, and God has inspired him to do it, then God, when He sees fit, will give the increase and provide labourers for the harvesting. He himself must be glad and joyful: despondency unfits a man to be God's servant and leads him into deadly sin. These arguments have no effect; still less has the hermit's suggestion that the cause of his failure lies in his own system. If, he says, the *Art* is despised, may not that be because the Christian verities cannot in fact be proved by argument?

> That which thou dost ask,
> That faith be prov'd by reason, is a task
> Impossible.
> . . . If we could clearly prove our faith,
> Merit were lost.
> . . . The truth of God being infinite,
> Man's understanding reaches not its height;
> Much must be hidden from our mortal sight;
> Wherefore thine arguments are worthless quite.

Ramon protests passionately. If the Faith cannot be proved, why should Christians teach it? Does God, Who has given us understanding, expect us to follow a law which runs clean counter to it? He, Ramon, does not claim that man's little mind can comprehend the infinite, but only that sufficient of that infinite is granted to its comprehension to enable a man to be a Christian and to love and serve God.

The hermit now shifts his ground. It is useless, he

asserts, to preach to Mahomet's followers, both because
of their obstinacy and of the difficulty of their language.
Ramon replies that, as to the first point, Mohammedans
could be converted with comparative ease:

> If to them men for disputations went
> And proved their faith by force of argument.

As to the learning of Arabic, that is quickly done, and
quickly it should be done.

The hermit disagrees:

> Ramon, when world-conversion God shall will,
> His Holy Spirit wisdom shall instil.
> With gifts of tongues His servants He shall fill
> As in the Apostles' days, so shall He still.

"No," replies Ramon, "God has ever willed the conversion of the world, giving men freedom to choose between good and evil." But the hermit is persistent. It
were better to "retain what has already been won" than
to go abroad to heathen lands where so many have met
with failure. Let Ramon betake himself to some quiet
spot, where he may pass the rest of his life in well-earned
tranquillity.

It becomes increasingly clear, as the poem proceeds, that
the hermit represents Ramon's lower self. He is rebuked
for his suggestion, sternly. "And what of the God-given
Art?" enquires Ramon. "Can I allow it, after all this
labour, to be lost? What shall I say to its Giver when He
calls me to my last account?" For answer, the hermit
begins to attack the *Art*. If it be indeed of value, how is it
that it was unknown to olden philosophers? And, if it be
of God, why do you repine? In that case, whether you
yourself live or die matters little:

> Its virtue can by no device be kill'd,
> For all God gives is perfectly fulfill'd.

This point in the discussion seems in one sense to mark the climax of the poem. Hereafter the hermit is less the doubling of Ramon's own personality, and more the individual opposed to his convictions and ideals. Unfortunately, the line of argument which he takes is highly unsympathetic. What God does is just. If He wills that the heathen perish in Hell, we must not on this account be disconsolate. Ramon becomes impatient with such arguments, and, did not courtesy forbid him to do so, would break off the conversation. Instead, he listens while the hermit develops his theory of Divine election. The discussion becomes more acrid.

> Hermit, hadst thou a better education,
> Thou might'st indeed discuss predestination,

cries Ramon. To which the hermit:

> Thou wouldst not pine, wert thou in hope well school'd,
> If the whole world should be unjustly rul'd.

They cease at last to argue, both realizing that it is useless to continue, and the hermit, despairing, no doubt, of one whom he holds to be in such error, resumes his task of consolation. Thereupon Ramon, for his part, resumes his plaints, in lines which, in their original, throb with the eloquence of suffering:

> Not greatly, hermit, should a man complain
> If children, lands and wealth are from him ta'en,
> And God be pleased to send his body pain.
> But, if the name of God be had in vain,
> Blasphemed, despised, forgotten, then 'tis plain
> Nor God nor man unmovèd can remain.
> Know'st thou not how for God's sake I have lain
> In grievous plight, waiting but to be slain,
> Pluck'd by the beard and curs'd with vile disdain,
> Yet patiently enduring every bane?
> How can I any comfort hope to gain
> When, despite all, no nearer comes God's reign?

We need not pursue the debate to its inevitable close. As so often happens in *Blanquerna*, the devil's advocate is converted by little more than the contagion of the angels. Ramon triumphs; and we leave the hermit begging his forgiveness:

> " I pray thee, sir, my grievous fault condone.
> Henceforth would I be sad with thee alone.
> Ah, Truth, Devotion, Love! Say, whither are gone
> The thanks and praise that should to God be done? "
> Then to the vanquish'd hermit went Ramon,
> Gently he kiss'd him, and they wept as one.[1]

Apart from its literary merits—the picturesqueness of the descriptions, the dramatic force of the dialogue, the vigour of the attack—the *Desconort* has a unique interest as a chapter of its author's autobiography. We hear from his own lips, not only the story of his past, but his ideals, his projects, his desires, his beliefs, his doubts, his questionings and his fears, in the proportion—and this is the most important point of all—which they occupied in his own mind at the time.

It gives us a most vivid picture of the Fool of Love as old age was creeping upon him. Miramar had been built: it had also been abandoned and destroyed. If its founder had been befriended by kings and emperors, kings and emperors had also forsaken him. From his travels over half the known world, a Divine knight-errant, not knowing yet of the martyr's crown which awaited him, he returned again and again to the palace of his ideals in the world's centre, Rome, the door of which, slowly opening, revealed each time disillusion. As we turn the pages of the poignant chronicle of his shattered hopes, we begin to see him as a pathetic figure, even as a tragic one. But he was too robust and vital a character for such an impression to be possible

[1] *R.L.*, pp. 256-65.

against Siger of Brabant, Boetius of Dacia, Bernier of Nivelles and other leading Averroists. In 1277, four years before Siger's assassination, matters were brought to a head by the formal condemnation of no less than two hundred and nineteen propositions extracted from the heterodox leaders' teaching. Among them we find some of Averroes' chief doctrines, and others held not by himself but by his followers. There was the theory that one creature only —a first Intelligence—is produced directly by God, and that all other creatures are produced by intermediaries. There was that form of fatalism in which celestial bodies are made to determine terrestrial happenings, and a moral determinism familiar to later ages. Another of these doctrines, strongly opposed by the schoolmen, was the unity of human intellect, and an even more abhorrent theory was that of the two truths—the idea that what is true in theology may be false in philosophy, and *vice versa*.

A historian as impartial in the matter as Renan has described Ramon Lull as the hero of the crusade against Averroism. He began his activities, in February 1298, by producing a book with a title several lines long, in which, under the usual allegorical form, he justified the action of the Bishop of Paris. In one of his characteristic forests he meets a thirteenth-century Socrates, who undertakes to justify the beliefs which had been censured. Lull, nothing loth, proposes a philosophical debate on the articles of certain Averroistic philosophers which had been condemned by the Bishop of Paris. This is duly held and described in detail: when it is over, each party, as is the usual proceeding in such cases, claims the victory.

But, in October of the same year, a very much finer work was " finished by Ramon, near the city of Paris "—the *Tree of the Philosophy of Love*. Though more unequal in merit than most of his major works—in places prolix,

involved and frankly dull—it is as delightful and as profit-
able a book to dip into as Ramon ever wrote. It moves
in various and varied mediums—in maxim and allegory,
subtlety and simplicity, poetry and prose, exposition,
meditation and prayer. Never for long is it devoid of
grace and charm, nor of the fervour of a single-minded
lover of beauty, wholly devoted to God. Though not a
mystical treatise, it abounds in the raw material of all
mysticism—an unquenchable desire.

In the heart of his "fair wood" Ramon descries a lady,
clad in costly apparel, making great lamentation. She is
Philosophy-of-love, and her sorrow is great because men
court her sister Philosophy-of-knowledge, make "many
books and many arts" in the sciences, and neglect entirely
the art of love. Her complaint inspires him to write a new
book on the philosophy of love, which he proceeds to plan
in characteristically artificial fashion. It is the latter part
of the book—translated into English as the *Tree of Love*—
which chiefly appeals to modern readers. The Lover of
the story falls grievously sick and is visited by the Physician
of love, who

found that the Lover had need of a medicine which should
give him frenzy, that love might cause him to speak as a fool,
for they that speak of love in manners most like to those of
fools are they that are in truth the sanest. So the Physician
compounded a medicine of the roots of the tree of love, that
it might be very potent, and gave it to the Lover, bidding him
drink it for love of his Beloved.[1]

The Lover drinks the potion, but finding himself "in
straiter travail of love than heretofore", cries out that the
physician has poisoned him, and bids his servants find him
another physician and an antidote. But the antidote only
"multiplies his frenzy"; so the Lover declares that he will

[1] *T.L.*, p. 35.

" flee from so evil a physician and such evil servants, and go away to live in a forest " where he will hear nothing of his Beloved and so be cured of his sickness. Accordingly, that night, while the physician and the servants are sleeping, he makes his escape.[1]

After some time he is recaptured, and bound to his Beloved " with many cords of love . . . that he might not flee from Him, nor from the trials of love ". He is likely to be condemned to death, but the Lady of love pleads for him, and he is allowed Life-of-love as an advocate, who, following the fashion of the medieval Courts of Love, pleads against Death-of-love in his favour. Judgment is given against him, and he makes his confession, draws up his testament and utters a humble prayer of great beauty to the Beloved, " for by prayer there comes from Beloved to Lover grace and pardon ". But when all is done, and he lies down to die, Death-of-love is found to have no power over him, and it is only by taking him to the Holy Land, and showing him the Holy Places, that the enemies into whose power he has been delivered can cause him to die from the very strength of his devotion.[2]

Then comes a particularly beautiful description of the Lover's burial:

When the Lover was dead, the servitors of love bathed and washed him with the tears that he had shed for love's sake, the which tears had been laid up by Remembrance-of-love; and they wrapped him in fair white samite, whereby it was signified that he had been cleansed from his sins. Over that white samite they spread another cloth of samite that was crimson, the which was to signify that the Lover was a martyr for love's sake. And over the samite of crimson they spread samite of gold, in significance that the Lover had been proved and had remained ever loyal to his Beloved and to love. After

[1] *T.L.*, p. 36.   [2] *T.L.*, pp. 36-66.

this they set the body of the Lover upon a bed of patience and humility, and, bearing candles lighted at the flame of love, they brought it into the church of love.

When the body of the Lover was brought into the church of love, the prayers were sung by Life-of-love, who was vested in sanctity and virtues, for the soul of the Lover had departed to the true life, to be for ever with his Beloved. The Roots of love made their responses to Life-of-love, and the servitors of love bare the candles.

Many and long and solemn were the prayers that were recited at the burial of the Lover, and Life-of-love preached, and praised the Lover greatly, and recounted the griefs and the trials which he had borne as a good and loyal lover. The ladies and the servitors of love wept sorely when they heard the many praises of the Lover which the preacher of love recounted, and they had very great sorrow and grief at the death of the Lover, whereto they had been accessory and consenting.

In a fair coffin, wrought of love, glory, truth, humility and piety, the servitors of love placed the body of the Lover, and the palls, the candles and the bed they gave to the poor who begged for alms, for the sake of love, more than for their necessities of eating and sleeping.[1]

The Lady of love now chooses a new Lover, who, with his fellow-lovers, attempts to arouse men to love God by making a journey of praise throughout the world. But their experiences are unhappy. First, they visit a church where " many men sang the honours of the Beloved ", but " even as they sang they thought upon sins which they were to commit ". Next, they see " a great school wherein a master taught many disciples ", but some of these disciples desire learning for unworthy motives. A monastery yields no better result: one monk is a slave to pride, and another to hypocrisy, while at the royal court, where the king is to all appearances just and honourable, his motives are unworthy and he " dishonours the Beloved in his

[1] *T.L.*, pp. 66-8.

intention ". Then the Lover and his companions go through the capital, and find that all the Beloved's commandments are broken openly. And, taking counsel in a " fair meadow " outside the city, they decide that their desire is " to leave the world, and to be no more among men, but rather to dwell in the woods with birds, beasts and trees, for these dishonour not the Beloved ".[1]

But beneath the conclusion of the narrative we may read the feelings of a man, not of the cloister, but of the world, who is speaking to us in his own character:

Then the Lover and the ladies of love entered a forest, and found therein a pilgrim returning from his pilgrimage, who asked them whither they were going. The Lover and the ladies of love recounted to him the intention for the which they were leaving the world and purposed to dwell in the forest. The pilgrim rebuked them sternly, saying that they should return to the world to live among men, and not be idle, to the end that the Beloved should have servants who should rejoice in His honours, and should bring Him honour, and whensoever He is dishonoured should have grief and sadness. " And have ye consolation," said the pilgrim, " by reason of the justice which the Beloved will work in the world to come upon them that in this world do Him dishonour. For none will have defence against the Beloved, neither will any be able to deny or hide from Him the dishonour which they have done Him. Return ye therefore to the world, and look to it that the Beloved may have many good servants and that the world may have truth and be in good estate."[2]

During the late summer of the year 1299, a great desire came to Ramon to return for a time to his native island, which he appears not to have seen for something like twenty years. A year previously, through the influence of Pope Boniface, the kingdom of Majorca had been restored to the unhappy James, on condition that he held it from his nephew of the same name, who was now King of

---

[1] *T.L.*, pp. 81-99.   [2] *T.L.*, pp. 99-100.

F

Aragon, just as he had previously held it from Peter. It was natural that his old tutor should think of going to see him there.

He went first, however, to Barcelona, in order to take advantage of a licence which had just been given him (in a document still extant) to enter all the synagogues and mosques of the royal dominions for the purpose of preaching the true Faith. Strange as such a permission may now seem, it was by no means unusual. Throughout the thirteenth century, owing mainly to the zeal of the Dominicans, attempts of the kind were continually made to convert Jews and Moslems. In 1263, for example, James the Conqueror had ordered his Jewish subjects to sit at the feet of the Friars Preachers, and in the same year had himself listened to a debate, held at Barcelona, between a converted Jew, appropriately baptized Paul, who had entered the Order of St. Dominic, and a rabbi of Gerona. Five years later, complaints that the Jews of Barcelona were being ill-treated led to their being granted a royal dispensation from attending Christian missions outside their own quarter: they were also allowed to refuse to admit into their synagogues more than ten Christians at a time in the company of a Christian preacher. These and other incidents make it clear how ordinary was his request: indeed, it seems likely that the permission accorded him was less than he had expected; for, says the contemporary biography, "when he had besought the said king concerning certain things of utility to the holy Catholic faith and had seen that it profited him nothing, he then returned to Majorca ".[1]

Here, too, as a quarter of a century earlier, he "laboured continually with disputations and sermons to convert the Moors who were there ";[2] but suddenly, into the midst of

[1] *C.B.*, p. 30.   [2] *Ibid*. Cf. p. 21, above.

his activities, there burst news which filled him with a fresh enthusiasm. The Khan of Tartary, a monarch friendly to Christianity, was said to have conquered Syria; and, if this were so, argued Ramon, there would certainly be the fullest freedom for Christians to preach in yet another Moslem land. Impulsive as ever, he lost no time in sailing for Palestine, but, on calling at Cyprus, he found that the news was incorrect. The Khan had, it was true, gained a victory over the joint forces of Egypt and Syria, and Boniface VIII had gone so far as to make a public prediction of the accomplishment of what Christian crusades had failed to effect—the deliverance of the Holy Places from the unbelievers. But, unfortunately, the Khan had not consolidated his victory when he had been forced to leave in order to quell a rebellion in Persia, whereupon the Syrians revolted and their King regained his throne.

The journey, in those days, from Majorca to Cyprus was a long one and even Ramon must for the moment have felt hopelessly frustrated. But he soon recovered sufficiently to turn the misfortune to good account. Catalans, always great travellers, were as well known in Cyprus as in North Africa, and he found no difficulty in getting the King's permission to preach to unbelievers here as he had done there. After a stay of some months, marked chiefly by an unsuccessful attempt to poison him, he made a visit to the mainland and then returned in a leisurely fashion, by way of Rhodes and Malta, to Majorca.

It was in the year 1302 that he arrived home again, and he was on the point of attaining his threescore years and ten, yet there is no indication that he was ready or anxious for retirement. On the contrary, he was never more active than in the next five years, which he spent between Palma, Barcelona, Montpellier, Lyons and Genoa, preaching and writing incessantly, especially in Montpellier, which had become to him a second home. Of the numerous books which belong to this period, only one calls for description, the *Liber* (or *Libellus*) *de Fine*, which has the attractive quality of being much more personal than most of the books which he wrote in Latin.

It was evidently written in a period of deep depression. Its preface, after lamenting the preponderance of unbelievers in the world, describes the author's renunciation of his possessions, and the efforts which he has made to excite princes, cardinals and popes to missionary zeal. He has written many books to expose the errors of unbelievers: this book shall be the last of all, hence its name. " I can do no more than I have already done," is his cry. " I find none who will lend me in any way effective help. So I set down my arguments in final form and order, once and for all, that on the Day of Judgment I may stand guiltless and unafraid in this respect before the company of Heaven— nay, before God Himself."

The first section of the book expounds Ramon's ideas on preaching and debating with unbelievers and the institution of colleges for the training of missionaries. The second deals with armed crusades—a subject which he continually treats, though seldom at great length—and with another of his pet ideas, the unification of the military Orders. The third comprises a fresh commendation of the *Ars Magna*. But the true theme of the book, from beginning to end, is that of the *Desconort*—the author's disillusion. Take these training colleges, he says: why are they not established? Surely not because of the trivial cost: let the Holy Father and the Cardinals but set them up and they will be abundantly rewarded. Take crusades: why have all the boasted exploits of the Christians failed to drive the Moslems from the Holy Places? Let the military Orders unite under a chosen leader and let a new crusade start from Spain and proceed by way of Ceuta and Tunis to Palestine.

Amid all this matter-of-fact planning, the note of rhetoric is not lost. There is a touching description of the sad state of Jerusalem, made more vivid by contrast with the splendour of papal Rome. Oftentimes has Ramon himself seen the Holy Father, surrounded by his Cardinals, saying Mass in St. Peter's and praising Christ our Lord. But there is "another altar": one of its two lamps is broken, and its city is desolate, though it is excellent above all cities else. Alas, that we allow this—we who are called Christians!

Then, turning from the depressing past and the uncertain present to the glorious future, Ramon breaks forth into eulogy and prayer:

Ah, devout and faithful King, whosoever thou art, what honour will be thine in Heaven and upon the earth, when thou shalt present thy son for the accomplishment of this task, so good, so great and so worthy. How great will be thy joy when thou seest this thy son raised to this lofty dignity and highly exalted with honour! . . . Ah, Jesus Christ our Lord God, descend Thou among us, complete and perfect this work and bring it to the holy end which Thou desirest.[1]

The *Liber de Fine*, then, is a book not only of disillusion but of desire and defiance, a book that marks, not an end, but a fresh beginning. Hardly had Lull completed it than he was off to visit the Pope again. But not Boniface, who ten years before had sent him away from Rome empty. Both Boniface and his short-lived successor were dead, and in June 1305 a Frenchman, an Archbishop of Bordeaux, was elected Pope as Clement V. Starting his reign by deciding to be crowned in Lyons, instead of in Rome, Clement

[1] *R.L.*, pp. 316-19.

left Bordeaux in August and stayed for four days at Montpellier, where he met the Kings of Aragon and Majorca. At this interview, so Lull himself tells us, the conversation turned on the possibilities of a new crusade, for which King James of Aragon offered " his person, his throne and his treasure ", afterwards presenting Clement with a copy of the *Liber de Fine*. " And of this I am certain," adds Lull, " for I was there."[1]

Subsequently he followed Clement to Lyons, and in all probability witnessed the coronation, which took place in November. Soon after his arrival, he had audience of the Pope, and put to him his case for the establishment of colleges, as well as his military projects, with all the eloquence of one who feels success, long deferred, to be within his reach at last. But once again he failed to arouse any enthusiasm; not for the first time he had chosen the wrong moment. Philip, King of France, a friend of Clement's from his youth, had been at daggers drawn with the ambitious Boniface, and saw in Clement's election a chance of taking revenge on the memory of his former foe. While the King was demanding that the name of Clement's great predecessor should be erased from the Papal records, his body disinterred, his bones burned and their ashes flung to the winds, it would be hard enough for the Pope to give his attention to projects for the teaching of Oriental languages, to say nothing of taking practical steps to carry them into effect.

In all probability Ramon Lull underestimated or was ignorant of the difficulties which beset the way of the newly crowned Pope when he presented himself before him. If so, the shock of unexpected failure would have been the greater. Intense depression was followed by a not unnatural exaltation of spirit, under the influence of which

[1] *R.L.*, p. 321.

he shook off the dust of Lyons from his feet and, after a
short return to Majorca, went to Paris.

Each time that he visited the great University he was
more and more sought after and revered. But, since he
had last been there, a new and resplendent star had
appeared in the academic firmament: Duns Ṣcotus, a young
Franciscan, whom rumour credited, as it had credited
Ramon, with supernatural illumination, and who, at the
command of the General of his Order, had left throngs of
pupils at Oxford to go and teach his philosophy at the
Sorbonne.

Of his first meeting with Ramon, the story is told that
the white-bearded apostle was sitting at the feet of the
young teacher, giving clear signs, perhaps absent-mindedly,
of his agreement with, or dissent from, different points of
the lecture. Duns Scotus, thinking to rebuke what he took
to be the ignorant presumption of an old man whom he
had not seen in his audience before, turned upon him with
a question ridiculously elementary :

" *Dominus*, quae pars? "[1]

To which Ramon, in no way surprised into silence, calmly
answered :

" Dominus non est pars, sed totum."[2]

And his eulogists have it that, as he spoke, he stood up in
the hall and silenced both lecturer and audience with
a magnificent improvisation upon the perfection of the
Divine Nature.

Early in 1307, Ramon set out from Paris upon a second

[1] " What part (*i.e.*, of speech) is *Dominus* (Lord)? "
[2] " The Lord is no part, but the whole."

African mission, landing at Bugia, a town about one hundred miles east of Algiers.

As we have seen, he was often unfortunate in his choice of moments for entrances upon the stage of publicity. He could hardly have selected a worse time for his new campaign than this. There had been war in North Africa: Tlemcen was suffering the final stages of an eight years' siege; Bugian troops were fighting Tunis and had captured Constantine; Algiers had just elected to declare its independence and was fighting hard to defend it. Added to all this, for more than a year a religious reformer called Saâda had been attacking Mohammedan orthodoxy in the city of Bugia and the surrounding country, and contemporary accounts point to the extreme inflammability, at the time, of the popular temper.

How much of all this Ramon knew when he left Europe one cannot say; but he added fuel to the popular fire by the tactless way in which he began his mission. A Fool of Love indeed! "When he was in the midst of the market-place," says the contemporary biography, "forgetful of the peril of death, he began to cry in a loud voice: 'The law of the Christians is holy and true, and the sect of the Moors is false and wrong, and this am I prepared to prove.'" Again and again he repeated this daring challenge, until a furious mob, already exasperated by one religious agitator, had gathered around him tumultuously, intent upon his death.[1]

They seem, however, to have been prudent enough to ask the authorization of the Kadi, or chief judge of the city, who, desirous of seeing the picturesque, white-bearded orator for himself, had him brought before him. What happened next is described by the contemporary biography:[2]

[1] *C.B.*, pp. 33-4.   [2] *C.B.*, pp. 34-5

"How is this," enquired the Kadi, "that thou hast committed folly so great, attempting to impugn the law of Mahomet, when it is certain that every one that impugns it shall die a cruel death? "

"The true servant of God," answered Ramon, "must fear no peril of death in showing forth the truth to infidels who are in error and bringing them into the way of salvation."

"True," replied the Kadi. "But which is that law that is erroneous and false? Is it of the Christians or of the Moors? I would fain hear thy arguments, if thou hast any, whereby thou dost prove thy law. Tell them to me, for I will hear them willingly."

"That pleases me," returned Ramon. "Give me a place that is convenient wherein are thine own learned men, and I will prove to thee, by necessary reasons, that the law of the Christians is holy and true."

A time and a place were thereupon appointed and the debate was held. Part of it has come down to us—as reported, of course, by Ramon himself: some passages in which he attempted to " prove the Holy Trinity ".[1] At this " lofty reasoning ", however, the biography reports, the Kadi " marvelled ", and " answered never a word, but commanded that he should be thrown forthwith into prison ". Then the fury of the waiting mob broke out, and they demanded leave to stone him. This, however, the Kadi forbade, saying that in due time a trial in proper form would take place; " for," explains the chronicler, " he desired that he should be condemned to death by trial and judgment."

So the mob could only show its wrath with Ramon by insulting him as he was led away to prison. Some belaboured him with sticks, others hurled stones at him, others struck him with their fists, and those who could get near

[1] C.B., pp. 35-6.

enough pulled at his long white beard. The Kaḍi's officers
did their best to protect him, but without much success,
and it can only have been a relief to the venerable preacher
when he found himself safely in the foul closet of his
prison, and loaded with heavy chains. It was but a literal
counterpart of the mystical experience which he had
described allegorically more than once:

Imprisoned was the Lover in the prison of Love. Thoughts,
desires and memories held and enchained him lest he should
flee to his Beloved. Griefs tormented him; patience and hope
consoled him. And the Lover would have died, but the
Beloved revealed to him His Presence, and the Lover
revived.[1]

Meanwhile, the Kadi took counsel with the other
authorities as to Ramon's fate, and they resolved by a
majority to put him on his trial, to kill him if he was found
to be a man of learning and therefore dangerous, but, if he
seemed to be a harmless fanatic, to let him go. One of the
Moors who was present at this council, however, had known
something of him at Tunis. "Beware!" he said to them.
"Make him not to come here before you all, for he will
bring against our law such arguments as it will be impossible
to answer." The warning was heeded, and a new opinion
now found favour, that the most politic action would be
to transport him to another dungeon, more loathsome still,
where he would probably die from his privations. The
thing was done; but, before any ill effect could ensue, the
Catalans and Genoese, who traded as freely in Bugia as in
Tunis, petitioned that their fellow-Christian might have
better treatment. They, no doubt, or some of them, were
among the most influential of the Christian merchants, and
their prayers prevailed.

In another and "more tolerable" prison Ramon

[1] *B.L.B.*, 168.

remained for about six months—approximately from May to November 1307. He seems to have been treated there with real kindness, and allowed, not only to receive visitors, but to debate with well-disposed Moors upon the very subjects for discussing which in public he was deprived of his liberty. " Each day," says the contemporary biography:

Each day came the Moors, praying him to be converted to the law of Mahomet, and offering him infinite treasures, honours and women. But he, like one that was established on immovable rock—that is, in the fervent love of his Master Jesus—answered them, saying: " And if ye yourselves will renounce this your false sect, and will believe in the Holy Name of Jesus, I promise you eternal life and treasures that will never fail you."[1] .

The curious result of these debates which Lull, while in captivity, carried on with his adversaries, the chief of them being a " learned Moor named Hamar ", was an agreement, proposed by Lull himself, by which either side was to compose a book proving his law to be true, copies of each book to be sent to the chief authorities in Christendom and Islam. Hamar's only stipulation was that he should be allowed to begin, for—he naïvely added—his arguments would be found unanswerable. Lull readily consented, and set about his part of the task with alacrity, thinking that here at last was a chance for him to get a full and adequate hearing. He began his book in Arabic, sending the Kadi a summary of it when it was nearing completion, as a basis for his adversaries' portion. But Satan — as the contemporary biography phrases it—saw that this would never do, for " along that road all these souls would go to Paradise ". The enemy of truth arranged, therefore, that the King of Bugia, who was at that time in Constantine, not far away, should come to hear of the matter and order that Ramon

[1] C.B., p. 39.

should be expelled immediately, and, if he returned, be put to death.[1]

This, however, was not the end of the adventures of that second African mission. He was placed on board a ship bound for Genoa, strict orders having been given to the captain that he was not to land him until they reached Christian territory. As they approached Pisa, a storm sprang up, the ship was wrecked some ten miles from land, and a handful of the passengers alone escaped in a boat. Among them was Ramon. He had been able to save nothing, either of his books or of his clothing. Helpless and destitute he landed, and in some fashion made his way from the shore to Pisa.[2]

By this time he must have been about seventy-five years old. In the course of a few months he had gone through two voyages, a shipwreck, a trial for his life, a long imprisonment under the foulest conditions, and maltreatment, at least once, at the hands of a mob. But neither his body nor his mind was disposed to rest; still less was his indomitable will. "Albeit very ancient of days," remarks the biography, "the said reverend master ceased not to serve his Creator."[3]

[1] *C.B.*, pp. 36-40.   [2] *C.B.*, p. 40.   [3] *C.B.*, p. 41.

VI

THIRD AFRICAN MISSION

*Love is an ocean; its waves are troubled by
the winds; it has no port or shore. The Lover
perished in this ocean, and with him perished
his torments, and the work of his fulfilment
began.*
                                    —*B.L.B.*, 235

IN PISA—need one say it?—this marvellous old man
betook himself once more to writing. Retiring, for a period
of tranquillity, to a monastery not far from the city, he drew
up a Latin account of his " disputation " with Hamar and
then completed a new exposition of his *Art* which he had
begun at Lyons over two years before, and, unless he had left
the manuscript behind him when sailing for Bugia, must have
been compelled to recommence from memory. This done,
he composed "many books beside ",[1] one of which is dedicated to the "Chancellor, Rector, Dean and other chief
members" of the University of Paris.[2] The dedication
alludes to the abortive interview which Ramon had had
with the Pope at Lyons and begs them ever to bear in mind
his three requests and to help him to obtain their fulfilment.

But at Pisa, as elsewhere, Ramon did much more than
write books. He seems to have found here the spirit that
more than once he had looked for in vain at Rome. He
proposed to the City Council "that it would be good if
certain of their citizens became knights of Jesus Christ to
conquer the Holy Land".[3] Most probably he knew that

---

[1] *C.B.*, p. 41.   [2] *R.L.*, p. 335.   [3] *C.B.*, p. 41.

the Grand Master of the Hospitallers was discussing a new
Crusade with Clement V and intended that the Pisans whom
he recruited should join it. He would certainly not have
been disappointed in them. They gave his proposal a warm
welcome, and sent him to the Papal Court with letters of
recommendation and assurances of their support to bear
to the Pope and the Cardinals. On his way there, about
May 1308, he made a brief halt at Genoa, where he had
received much kindness, and here he was welcomed more
cordially still: many devout persons offered freely to help
him and collected over thirty thousand florins.

Armed with letters, promises and money, Ramon went
boldly forward. Soon after being crowned at Lyons,
Clement V had decided to fix his court at Avignon, and he
would have found himself in quite a French environment
when he took up his residence there, far from the quarrel-
some Italians of his day, whom he neither trusted nor understood. Towards Avignon, then, Lull journeyed, but first
he went to Montpellier, which drew him, in old age as
in youth, irresistibly. Throughout the winter he wrote
steadily, completing about one book each month until in
March 1309 he decided to continue his journey. The last
thing he wrote before he went was a *Book on the Acquisition
of the Holy Land*, addressed to the Pope, and aiming no
doubt at following up his successes in Pisa and Genoa. In
this book he outlined the expected course of such a crusade
as he had been preaching, and such as Clement also was
meditating at this very time. Lull's idea now is that, since
the Christian hosts have more galleys than the Saracens, the
holy war should begin on sea. Once the Christians are
masters of the ocean, they can attack by land. From Con-
stantinople a Christian army will devastate Syria. This
accomplished, to subdue Egypt will be comparatively easy,
especially if the parallel crusade, which Lull has always

yearned for, can be carried on in Spain and Northern Africa with Granada and Ceuta as its objectives. This is the argument of the first part of the book. Alas, for Ramon's hopeful plans and easy rhetoric! These things were never to materialize. No doubt they might have done so had petty jealousies and rivalries been swallowed up in the ocean of love. But that was not the way of fourteenth-century Europe.

The two latter parts of Lull's book, which discuss missionary work, contain very little that is new to us. He builds his three language schools light-heartedly at Rome, Paris and Toledo, and with a wave of his *Ars Magna* disperses all the arguments of faithless and zeal-less Christians who see a lion in the missionary's way everywhere.

Once more, however, Ramon's meeting with the Pope ended in disillusion. "When he saw that he could accomplish naught," says the chronicler wearily, " he went away."[1] It was a hopeless time to press any kind of constructive proposal. The case against Boniface, to the introduction of which, on Philip's repeated insistence, Clement had reluctantly agreed, was just being heard, while the other question on which King and Pope were opposed—the suppression of the Templars—was being worked out at the same time by means of an investigation of charges against the Order. Nor did the Grand Master of the Hospitallers get very far with the Crusade as he had planned it. Several monarchs granted him their favour; galleys and provisions were collected; in Italy, France and Germany men and boys took the Cross in large numbers. In the spring of 1310, the Grand Master, with a numerous fleet, sailed thence for Rhodes, and on August 15 of that year, having picked up reinforcements at Cyprus, captured it. There, whether by misfortune or by design, the projected Crusade came to

[1] *C.B.*, pp. 42, 82.

an untimely end. The Knights Hospitallers became the Knights of Rhodes. And that was all.

Meanwhile, Ramon was in Paris again; and we may imagine that this latest disappointment was soon forgotten in the delight with which he found himself in greater request at the University than ever before. As he lectured upon his *Art*, says the biography," there came to hear him, not students alone, but also a great multitude of masters, who affirmed that (his) holy science and doctrine was corroborated not only by philosophical arguments, but also by the principles and rules of sacred theology ". If there were some who " averred that the holy Catholic faith could not be proved ", Ramon did not despair of converting them, but "made divers books and treatises " in which he combated their opinions.[1]

In Paris—for the last time, as it proved—Ramon stayed for over two years, from the spring of 1309 to the autumn of 1311. During that period he received not only the practical homage of crowded lecture-rooms, but also public testimony of a more durable kind. In 1310, on "the Tuesday after the octave of the Feast of the Purification " (February 10), a body of forty masters in the University drew up, at Ramon's request, and " of their own free will ", a statement approving a summary of the *Ars Magna* and styling it " good, useful and necessary, containing nothing contrary to the Catholic faith, but many things in support of the said faith ".[2] And this testimony was not only to be published, but to be repeated, literally and *viva voce*, to Master Raymundus Lull himself, by a deputation sent for the purpose to his own house. No doubt this testimonial was intended to strengthen the effectiveness of Lull's attacks on the

[1] *C.B.*, p. 42. Cf. also the longer account on p. 84.
[2] *R.L.*, p. 343.

Averroists, which he made continually, both in disputations and in his writings. It was Averroism, too, among other things, which took Ramon to the General Council of the Church, called by Clement largely to discuss the future of the Templars, and held at Vienne, a town between Avignon and Lyons.

Or was Averroism an excuse, rather than a reason? The old warrior was by now nearly eighty. Did he not perhaps feel that this might be his last chance to gain a fair hearing for the whole of his projects in what should be a tranquil and a sympathetic atmosphere? One would suppose so from a perusal of the *Petition of Ramon to the General Council*, which summarizes them all. Here he again suggests the establishment of missionary colleges in Rome, Paris and Toledo; advocates the unification of the military Orders in preparation for a new Crusade; and urges the intensification of war on Averroism. Then he turns to internal affairs: superfluous luxury must be uprooted from the Church and plurality of offices done away with. After this, with the inconsequence of an old man who in his time has seen many sides of life, he roams farther afield. A campaign must be started against Christian usurers; there must be more salaried judges, and the science of law, being "very prolix and diffuse", must be reduced to syllogisms. The science of medicine must be reformed by the exaltation of experience and experiment at the expense of authority. The dress and tonsure of the clergy must be changed: the tonsure should be uniform and the dress sober, economical and distinct from the attire of the layman. Most important of all, the *Petition* calls for the subsidizing of the new Crusade by secular princes, under penalty of excommunication, as well as by the utilizing of certain sources of ecclesiastical revenue, comprising a tithe of the Church's wealth.[1]

[1] *R.L.*, pp. 351-2.

G

In the Pope's inaugural address to the Council, which turned on the question of the Templars, the reconquering of the Holy Land and the reform of the clergy, one at least of Ramon's projects was referred to, and it is by no means improbable that his representations about the projected Crusade, as well as on the foundation of missionary colleges, carried some weight, though he was clearly less qualified to speak of the first matter than of the second. He appears to have remained at Vienne until the termination of the Council in May 1312, occupying his spare time with the writing of a number of books, of which by far the most interesting is the "Dispute of a Cleric and Ramon the fantastic", generally known by an abbreviation of its Latin title—*Phantasticus*.

This book, like the *Disputation with Hamar*, is probably a reproduction, or an expansion, of Lull's personal experiences. Two travellers are going to the Council: one is a cleric, named Peter; the other, Ramon, a layman. "I have often heard of you," says the cleric, "as a most fantastic person. Pray, what are you going to do at the Council?"

Ramon describes his ideals, whereat Peter the clerk laughs heartily. "I had heard of you as a fantastic man," he cries, "but now I know you as the most fantastic of the fantastic. Only a hopeless dreamer could conceive such schemes as these." "Let us consider that," says Ramon. "Perhaps I am less fantastic than you. We will relate each of us his life's history."

The clerk first tells his story, which is almost a picaresque novel in little. He was a peasant's son, and began his career by begging. Then he was enabled to study for Orders, graduated at the University in arts and law, became a priest and an archdeacon, collected many important benefices and has used the wealth which has accrued to him through these in helping his numerous relatives to live more comfortably and to better their social positions. He is followed on horseback by his three nephews, to each of whom he has given a rich benefice, and he is now bound for the Court, where the offer of an important bishopric awaits him. His servants and horses are numerous; his expenditure is on the munificent scale which befits his wealth. He, certainly, is not fantastic, but discreet and prudent.

Ramon replies to this autobiography with the story which we already know. "I have been married," he says, "and had children; I have been well-to-do, lascivious and worldly. Everything that I had in the world I have left that I might honour God, procure the greater good of my neighbour, and exalt our holy Faith. I have learned Arabic, and striven to convert the Moors. I have been bound, imprisoned and assaulted. For five-and-forty years I have laboured to move Christian princes and prelates that they may promote the common weal of the Church. Now I am old and poor, yet still I have the same purpose, and I trust that, with the grace of God, I may persevere therein even unto death. Does such a life as this seem to you fantastic? Let your conscience judge, as God Himself will judge you."

This simple and noble *apologia* is followed by a dispute between the two men as to which of their stories is the less fantastic. Peter the Clerk says that it is his, because he is the happier and the more honoured by men. Ramon replies that it matters not how troubled one's life is if the public good be served by it, illustrating his arguments freely from his own experiences. They part—in Lull's usual style —without being reconciled; and, indeed, reconciliation between the ideals of two such contrary types of man would hardly be credible.

As soon as the Council of Vienne was over, Lull returned to his native island, staying, for a short time only, at his favourite Montpellier, on the way. For once the stay must have had sorrowful memories for him; the unfortunate King James of Majorca, who so often had made the city his home, had died in Majorca a year previously. It is not hard to imagine Ramon's feelings at the loss of one who had been to him, in turn, pupil, master and sovereign, besides proving at all times a sympathetic friend and a constant, if too often an impotent, well-wisher. He had arrived at an age when new friends are made no longer, and it may well have been with a premonition of his own passing from this world that he visited the spots in Montpellier which he and his royal lord had known for more than half a century. After crossing to Palma, he would doubtless make a pilgrimage to James' grave in the new Cathedral, and to what had once been the munificent foundation of Miramar, now almost forgotten.

During this visit to Majorca, which lasted for rather more than a year, Ramon planned a third African mission, from which he seems to have suspected that he would never return. Before setting out, therefore, he turned his mind to some practical tasks. On April 26, 1313, like the Lover in one of his own books, he sent for a " faithful scrivener " and drew up a testament " concerning the things which he had held in trust for his Beloved ".[1] One such, a spiritual testament, he had indeed made already:

He bequeathed his body to the worms that they might devour it, and to the dust of the earth that the wind might scatter it, and none might remember it any more; for many a time had he adorned it and clothed it with fair garments that men might speak of it and he himself have in it vainglory.

He bequeathed his heart to desires and sighs, and his eyes, with their weeping and tears, to those lovers of the Beloved that do penance for love's sake; and he bequeathed to them likewise his imagination, to imagine therewith the wonders of

[1] *T.L.*, p. 49.

22123

the glory of his Beloved, and the pains of hell and the torments of the devils. And he bequeathed to his Beloved his memory, understanding and will. And he bequeathed to men that are sinners the fear which he had of his Beloved by reason of his sins.[1]

Now he turns his mind for a time to worldly things. His wife, apparently, had died, but his son and daughter, both named as beneficiaries, were still living. Among the bequests which deserve mention are legacies to both the Dominican and the Franciscan Orders, to various convents of women and to orphan children. Ten of his own works —they are mainly, though not wholly, those written during the past twelve months—he desires to have copied on vellum in Romance and Latin, together with a collection of his sermons: one copy, in Latin, is to be sent, "for the love of God", to a Carthusian monastery near Paris where he has often worked, and another copy to Genoa. Nor does he forget his earlier havens of refuge, for a coffer full of books which is in his son-in-law's house is bequeathed to the monastery of La Real, his association with which goes back some fifty years.

The remainder of his money, and such of his books and copies of books made by order of his executors as remain undisposed of, he bequeathes to his executors to distribute upon his behalf—"for the love of God, and for the good of my soul and of theirs"—wherever they think best. He makes characteristically loving provision for the future of those of his books that are to be given away. The church that accepts them is to place them in a chest, to secure them by means of a chain, and to allow any persons belonging to that church to see and read them when they desire. These provisions regarding his own works are the most interesting parts of the testament. Certainly Justice, Prudence and Charity were among his executors; and

[1] *T.L.*, p. 49.

many, both rich and poor, must have been the better for his dying as for his living. "He may have willed," remarks a commentator, "that the dust of his body should be scattered to the four winds, but he willed more effectively a scattering of the fruits of his ardent and irradiant spirit ".[1]

And what of Miramar? There is no evidence that he made, or contemplated, any effort for its restoration. One likes to think that he kept its memory green, as a man will keep the memory of his firstborn. But in six-and-thirty years his horizon had widened, and he had but recently seen the apparent fulfilment of those hopes of which Miramar had been but the germ. His legacy to the island was a "Lullian School", which at a later date developed into the *Estudi General*, or Lullian University, of Majorca.

Within a week or two of drawing up his testament, the octogenarian set off on his last journey. First, he went to Sicily—beginning a new book at sea and finishing it at Messina—where he wrote and preached incessantly for almost exactly a year. Then he went back, for a few weeks, to Majorca, and, in August 1314, set off thence towards Africa. Landing at Bugia, that city of baleful memories, he went on to the more hospitable Tunis, where James of Aragon sent him a letter of commendation to the King:

King, we make thee to know that we have understood that our subject Ramon Lull is in thy city of Tunis, wherein it pleases him to dwell and to be. Wherefore, King, since we are acquainted with the said Ramon, and know that he is a man that is good and learned and of upright life, and love him, we pray thee that it may be thy will and pleasure, for our honour, to have and to hold the said Ramon in thy grace, and for this we shall be greatly beholden to thee.

Perhaps as a result of this letter, Ramon's life at Tunis was for a time comparatively peaceful; his preaching tours

[1] *R.L.*, p. 366.

to the villages were devoid of incident and his disputations with learned men in the cities quite amicable. So quiet was his life, in fact, that his thoughts turned again to his writings, and we find him, in July 1315, addressing King James and begging him to arrange for a certain Fra Simó de Puigcerdà, a former pupil of his, to be sent to him, in order to help him translate into Latin some of his recent works, embodying his disputations with the Saracens. Are we to see in this request for a collaborator evidence that at the age of eighty-three Ramon at last found his powers failing him—his eyesight, perhaps, or his memory? It is impossible to say. All we know is that the King complied with his request.

Very little information has come down to us about these books which he was to translate, or indeed about any of the works which he wrote in Tunis. One of them is actually dedicated to the Mufti of that city, which, considering the nature of its contents, is eloquent evidence to the cordiality of Lull's relations with those whom he was striving to convert. An ancient tradition, which this dedication confirms, describes the white-bearded old apostle as being more successful in this mission than in any before. Among his converts, says one chronicler, were some of the most influential and learned Moors of the city.

Was it for this reason that the tolerance which had been accorded to him suddenly ceased? Or was it because he felt his work in Tunis to be ended that he undertook (as nearly all tradition asserts) the long journey westwards again to Bugia? Whatever the reason for which he went there, what happened on his arrival can be quickly told. Flinging caution to the winds—perhaps because of the impunity with which he had taught at Tunis, perhaps (who knows?) because he was as truly inspired now as ever he had been half a century before at Randa—the Fool of Love

went out boldly into the streets, proclaiming in a loud voice
the truth of the religion for which he had spent his life. A
hostile crowd, no less furious than any from which in the
past he had escaped, collected around him. Someone took
up a stone. The rest of the story followed quickly.

Unresistingly—nay, triumphantly—the aged Lover of
Christ suffered the cruel stones to work their will upon him.
The moment of his going hence had come—the moment for
which he had yearned, as a youthful convert, in his *Book
of Contemplation*, and had never shrunk from save when
forgetful of his Beloved. "Thy servant and subject, O
Lord," he had written in his youth, "has very great fear
of dying a natural death . . . for he would fain have his
death the noblest that is, namely, death for Thy love."[1]
He had his wish. It may be, as the legend has it, that his
assailants left him all but dead, and that two Genoese
merchants begged his body from the Civil Governor, and,
finding life in it, took it on board a Genoese boat that was
about to sail. If that story be true, Ramon gave back his
spirit to God as he came in sight of his native island; this
perhaps he would have desired above all, who had longed to
die in the very ocean of love. Or it may have been to a dead
body that those pious merchants rendered the last offices.
There is appropriateness in picturing the martyr, who had
fought for so many years that he had strength to fight no
more, sinking beneath the tempest of his adversaries' blows,
which " were to him as flowers, and as a bed of love ".[2]
Then it was that " the Beloved revealed Himself to His
Lover, clothed in new and scarlet robes ", that He
" stretched out His Arms to embrace him " and " inclined
His head to kiss him ".[3] Then, like the earliest Christian
martyr, the faithful soldier and servant had the last vision
of his earthly life, and with it the first glimpse of Paradise.

[1] *R.L.*, pp. 371-2.   [2] *B.L.B.*, 36.   [3] *B.L.B.*, 91.

VII

RAMON LULL TO-DAY

*Said the Lover: " O ye that love, if ye will have
fire, come light your lanterns at my heart; if
water, come to my eyes, whence flow the tears
in streams; if thoughts of love, come gather
them from my meditations."*

RAMON'S MARTYRDOM TOOK PLACE, so far as
can be determined, between the end of December 1315 and
the following March, in approximately the eighty-fourth
year of his age. His body, so tradition has it, was taken
from Palma harbour to the church of St. Eulalia, where his
parents lay, after which it was re-interred by the Franciscans
in their friary.

The last statement, at least, is true enough. In a chapel
of the beautiful church of San Francisco at Palma, the relics
of Ramon Lull still lie, and have lain, with one brief inter-
ruption, since the chapel was built in 1448, when, after
being exposed for an entire day to the veneration of the
faithful, they were solemnly placed at rest there. In 1915,
at the sexcentenary of his death, they were re-enclosed in
a coffin of cedar wood, on which was engraved part of the
wonderful epitaph of the Lover from the *Tree of Love*:

Here lies a Lover, who has died for his Beloved, and for
love . . . , who has loved his Beloved with a love that is good,
great and enduring . . . , who has battled bravely for love's
sake . . . , who has striven against false love and false
lovers . . . , a Lover ever humble, patient, loyal, ardent,

liberal, prudent, holy and full of all good things, inspiring many lovers to honour and serve his Beloved.[1]

Never for long without popular veneration is the body of one who to the people of Majorca,[2] if not in the eyes of the Church, is a blessed saint. We have followed that body, with due reverence, to its last resting place: let us now see what fate has befallen the work of its indomitable spirit.

Hardly was Lull in his tomb than there began to form about his head a double halo of sanctity and science. The cult both of the man and of his work began early in Majorca, thanks partly to a chance happening—the pre- servation of his sepulchre from destruction in a disastrous fire—which struck the popular imagination. The celebrity of his writings soon spread from Majorca and the Catalan mainland. But soon, too, there began a virulent opposition to his teaching which was to last for centuries. The arch-persecutor of his memory was the fourteenth-century Dominican Inquisitor, Nicholas Eymeric, a man whose re- markable energy and talents were accompanied by a degree of obstinacy and violence no less unusual. In his fierce and fanatical attempts to prove that Lull's works contained heresies we see something more than a perverted enthusiasm for the unity of the Church and an exaggerated individual enmity: we see a particular expression of the antagonism between two powerful religious Orders. The well-known story of Dominic's girding himself with Francis' cord to symbolize his desire for the unification of their two societies recurs almost tragically to the memory when one reads of the acrimony with which these societies fought over the man who in his lifetime knew both so well, was for so long drawn to the one, and eventually allied himself with the other.[3]

It was in 1366 that Nicholas Eymeric began his lengthy

[1] *T.L.*, pp. 68-9.   [2] *R.L.*, p. 375.   [3] *R.L.*, pp. 236-7, 268.

campaign against Ramon Lull, denying his sanctity and inspiration, reviling his reputation and character, describing him as a heretic, an ignoramus, and a necromancer, appealing against him to Gregory XI, whose chaplain he was, producing (in 1376) a condemnatory bull by that Pope now generally considered to have been a forgery, and extracting from Ramon's genuine and apocryphal works one hundred propositions which it was not difficult to brand as heretical. Menéndez y Pelayo, examining Eymeric's propositions, describes some of them as mere cavilling, others as drawn from pseudo-Lullian works generally but erroneously ascribed to the master, and others again as admitting quite clearly of two senses—the one heretical and the other orthodox. In this brief sketch an analysis of them can find no place; but the study of them has led to a general acceptance of Lull's orthodoxy, and there is now wide agreement with Menéndez y Pelayo's judgment upon his teaching: "audacious indeed, fraught with danger if you will, but assuredly not heretical." The charges, when first made, were taken very seriously, and over twenty of Lull's books examined, but without result. During the fifteenth century his teaching recovered all its old authority; the School on Mount Randa flourished as it had not done for generations; and in 1483 the principal teaching of "Lullian science" was transferred to the Majorcan University at Palma.

With the glorious dawn of the Renaissance many feebler lights, including that of Lullian teaching, were dimmed, but before the beginning of Spain's Golden Age it was again burning brightly. No less a person than Cardinal Cisneros was responsible for the introduction of Lull's doctrines into the renowned University of Alcalá, which he founded in 1508, appointing one of Lull's biographers, Nicolás de Pax, professor of Lullian science there (1518). Cisneros also formed a Lullian library and subsidized an edition of Lull's works. In every way, indeed, he was enthusiastic for him. "I have a great affection," he wrote on October 8, 1513, "for all the works of the Doctor Ramon Lull, Doctor most illuminate, for they are of great importance and utility; wherefore be assured that I shall continue to favour him in every way that I can, and shall labour that his works may be published and read in all the schools."[1]

At about this time began a revived interest in Ramon as a personality. The biographies written by Bouvelles and Pax in the sixteenth century, and by Seguí, Daça and the Irish friar, Luke Wadding, in the seventeenth, are known to all students. It is said on good authority, though without documentary proof, that Leo X, who was Pope from 1513 to 1521, beatified him, and under the advocacy of Philip II and Philip III of Spain a determined attempt was made to secure his canonization. Actually, it was not till 1847 that any misgivings about his beatification were removed by the confirmatory act of Pius IX. The possibilities of his canonization, however, must be considered remote—partly because the orthodoxy of his vast body of writing is not beyond question and partly because so little is known about his death that no one can prove him to have been a martyr for the Faith.

The eighteenth century witnessed a fresh persecution of Lullism, much, though not all, of which is again attributable to the Dominicans. Juan Díaz de la Guerra, a Dominican Bishop of Majorca, elected in 1772, initiated a feud which led to a series of pitched battles. He rifled the Lullian library of the College of Sapiencia; cancelled the feasts of Ramon Lull in the diocesan almanac; prohibited almsgiving for the cult, even confiscating the collection plates; seized portraits, images and manuscripts; forbade

1 *R.L.*, p. 383.

the use of the name Ramon Lull in baptism; and im-
pounded even the moulds, blocks and standing type of
printers when these bore any relation to the hated hero.
Against his fanaticism, Lull's adherents, who of course
grew steadily in numbers, could do little. What they could
do, however, they did, keeping guard over Lull's tomb lest
the Bishop should desecrate that also and complaining
bitterly and strongly to the King. They had some success:
a Royal Order arrived which prevented the conversion of
the Sapiencia into a hospice (1776); then came commands
(1777) that images and pictures of Lull which had been
removed should be replaced, and the excommunicate on
Lull's account should be reinstated; and about the same
time a boat arrived at Palma bearing the welcome tidings
that the Bishop had been promoted to the see of Sigüenza.

But at this very time Lullism was taking a fresh impetus
both in Spain and abroad. Sollier's study in the *Acta
Sanctorum* (1708), Salzinger's monumental edition of Lull's
Latin works (1721-42) and the *Vindiciae lullianae* (1778),
by Pasqual, the Abbot of Ramon's beloved La Real, have
been utilized by all later scholars. And with Pasqual began
a new orientation of Lullian studies, which, under the
modern critics Rosselló, Obrador, Alcover and Galmes—
the last still living—was to lead to a complete reversal of
values.

Until now it had almost seemed as if he who in life had
disputed without ceasing was to be the subject of disputes
for ever. While his work was in fashion, while the modes
of thought to which he was accustomed still prevailed, none
could say what would be his fate in the future. But the
very discrediting of the *Ars Magna* and its progeny opened
to its author the kingdom of immortality. One half of his
schemes, as we can see to-day, were fantastic visions and
of the other half the essential features have for so long been

accomplished that we can hardly imagine a time when they were considered daring reforms. Such upheavals of thought would have buried the work of a lesser man under their ruins. But actually it was the very edifices which he himself erected that obscured his real greatness. Men turned from his mathematical diagrams to his dynamic personality, from the Tree of Science to the Tree of Love.

How, then, do we regard Ramon Lull to-day? First of all, as a writer, both in Catalan and in Latin, of extraordinary fecundity. The vitality of his temperament, denied one form of expression principally by causes beyond his control, found an outlet in another form which none could forbid him; and the result is astonishing to consider. The Sicilian, Mariano Accardo Sículo, who was well known as a Lullist in the sixteenth century, makes him the author of three thousand works. Custurer quotes a more modest statement of Joan Llobet, a fifteenth-century Lullist, that he had read five hundred. Pasqual compiles a list of two hundred and fifty, which must be taken as a minimum. And there is nothing unusual in this; for the Latin genius has always tended less towards concentration than towards self-dispersal over a wide field of activity. We are concerned rather with quality than with quantity. Wherein lies Ramon Lull's greatness? What is there of permanent value in his writings? These are questions which have been answered in many different ways during the last six centuries. From the standpoint of to-day we can answer them best by looking back, first of all, over the period that has intervened since his death and taking stock of the claims that have been made for him.

Much of his vogue during the Middle Ages, and not a few of the extravagances uttered in his defence, can be traced to a belief that the *Ars Magna* would do what its author claimed for it; that, as he himself held, it was perfect and indestructible, being in no sense his own work, but directly and literally inspired by God. Some such belief as this underlies the foundation of the Lullian schools, lecture-ships and like institutions, and the opposition to Lull's writings by those who thought them heretical was all the fiercer because of the importance attached to them by their defenders. Strange as it may seem to us, there really were those who could take seriously the refrain:

Tres sabios hubo en el mundo,
Adán, Salomón y Raymundo.[1]

The reaction against these absurdities was bound to come. In due time the man who has been described as being "before Dante himself, the great popular philosopher of the thirteenth century"[2] was ridiculed for his philosophy, not only by polemists in Spain like Feijóo, but abroad, in mere allusiveness, by novelists like Rabelais and scientists like Francis Bacon. To-day Ramon's importance as a philosopher is only historical. He may be "in some re-spects one of the most remarkable figures in the history of medieval philosophy",[3] but he is principally remembered as one of the most curious and picturesque.

Nor is he taken more seriously as (if the usual sense of the term be adhered to) a theologian. His campaign against the Averroists, and his stalwart defence of the unity of philosophy and theology, excite our admiration still, but they excite nothing else, so far removed from us is their epoch. Ink, if not blood, was freely and unprofitably spilt over the question of whether or no Ramon exalted the understanding unduly and claimed that the truth of

[1] "There have been three wise men in the world: Adam, Solomon and Ramon." The lines were frequently quoted on both sides in the controversies of the eighteenth century.
[2] *R.L.*, p. 403.　　[3] *Ibid.*

revealed religion could be proved by intellectual processes without the aid of faith. To-day it seems clear enough that, whatever of heresy can be extracted from his writings by the method of isolating passages from their context, Ramon had not the slightest intention of despising or underrating the importance of faith. Again and again he declared its supremacy: faith, he declares, is necessarily higher than intellect, even as oil is higher than the water above which it floats. Far from desiring to make any opposition between the Articles and faith, he affirms that they cannot be proved without its aid. It is faith which illumines the understanding; or, to change the metaphor, the understanding mounts by means of it; or again, faith and understanding are a man's two feet, each being equally necessary to anyone who possesses both. Before understanding can function in these lofty spheres, the possibility of there being mysteries of religion must be known (which is the work of faith), and there must further be the "habit of faith", which comes from the grace of God, a predisposition towards belief, "a presupposition by faith that the fourteen articles can be proved". And, even if this be present, the kind of proof that can be urged is a proof *per aequiparantiam*: not absolute but relative—a process of argument which frequently is concerned only with what is congruent or "fitting"—a "*Demonstratio, sive Persuasio*", in no way appearing, as rationalistic proof would do, to limit God, but negatively of supreme importance, since no infidel can destroy it.

If the failure by missionaries and other teachers in Lull's day to make use of apologetics exasperated him into over-insistence upon their efficacy, the fact is not surprising. His general position on this important subject is that of St. Thomas Aquinas, who upheld apologetics and made use of "necessary reasons" to prove all but a few of the higher truths of Christianity. The differences between him and Ramon are partly of emphasis and partly of method. Ramon sought, on the one hand, to press the unbelievers as closely as he could towards acceptance of the doctrines of the Holy Trinity and of the Incarnation: perhaps, in his passionate antagonism to the much bruited belief that what was true according to faith could be false according to reason, and *vice versa*, he pressed them sometimes too far. On the other hand, he used his arguments too little for defence and too much for attack, for they were frequently negative rather than positive. Again, this is an excess of the enthusiast, readily pardonable by those who live in an age when so much love has grown cold. Whether or no Ramon stepped for a moment, now and then, beyond the boundary line of orthodoxy, is no longer a matter of prime importance: it is swallowed up by other considerations as the less is by the greater.

Another question which excited past ages, but which may now be considered as finally put to rest, is the long-debated one of whether or no Ramon was an alchemist. So great was his fame that for centuries after his death the works of others were foisted upon his reputation, both of set purpose, by men who were anxious that their writings should receive attention, and unconsciously, by critics who genuinely believed them to be his. It is understandable enough, in view of Ramon's interest in natural science, that some of these apocryphal writings should be treatises on alchemy. The surprising fact is that, in face of strong evidence to the contrary, they should ever have been attributed to him by serious critics. Fortunately the vast majority of Lullian scholars have taken a saner view, recognizing that Ramon himself, in works known to be genuine, repeatedly attacked the alchemists' pretensions — a fact which, apart from other considerations, is surely final. It

H

may be added that not a single alchemical work is attributed to Lull in either the contemporary biography or the contemporary catalogues, and that the earliest known manuscript of such a work dates only from the fifteenth century. The *coup de grâce* to the alchemical legend was given in 1870 by a Spanish scientist of repute, Luanco, and since that time few writers have upheld it.

These are some of the principal reasons for which Ramon Lull has been judged an immortal. They range from that which he himself alleged—that he was the divinely inspired exponent of a method for converting the whole world—to the preposterous and even ludicrous claims at which he would have been the first to be astonished. He is the discoverer of nitric acid, of a Great Elixir, even of America! " He has been represented as a troubadour, a disillusioned Don Juan, a naturalist, a jurisconsult, a musician, a mathematician, a chemist, a navigator, a theologian . . . as everything except what he was "[1]—as what he *was*, and is now recognized to be, in contradistinction from what he *did*, or possibly may have done.

Our remaining task, then, is to portray him as he was, and as he will probably appear to future generations: as a patriarch of Catalan literature; as a great personality; and as an outstanding active-contemplative, a typical Franciscan.

1. Many people who are knowledgeable about literature have no idea that Catalonia, centuries before her union with the other Spanish states, had a medieval literature comparable with any other in Europe. Only in the eighteen-thirties, after a sleep of three centuries, was Catalan, as a literary language, revived, and it was this renaissance that brought Lull into prominence as a leading writer of the Middle Ages. To him was largely due the fact that of

[1] *R.L.*, p. 409, n. 5.

modern European languages Catalan was the first to take a place beside Latin as the instrument of philosophy. He, and none other, was the herald of the glories of Catalan poetry. He, again, was the greatest precursor, if not actually the first, of that noble company of religious writers, ascetics and mystics both, who flourished during the Golden Age in Spain.

Having regarded Lull thus, and having set him upon a pinnacle which he fully deserved to occupy centuries before, it was essential for these Catalan writers, not only to produce in accessible form the works which justified their action, but to make their reasons for it explicit. Then it was that the extent of Lull's claims to immortality, from the standpoint of pure literature, came to light. His prose, at its best, is simple, naïve, unaffected, as beautiful as the language in which it is written and as direct in its appeal to the intellect as the thoughts which it expresses are to the heart. His verse, unequal indeed, but ranging over a great variety of metres and seldom unworthy of preservation, has much the same charm, with the added distinction of being in the purest Catalan, and less influenced by Provençal than that of most of his contemporaries at a time when Provençal influence everywhere was high. As a poet he is seldom at his best in verse media, but through both his verse and his prose the spirit of poetry shines clearly: the vividness of his allegories, the beauty of his symbolism, the lofty flights of his imagination—all this and more marks him out from his fellows, and, for a long time, from his Catalan followers. Further, as we have already suggested, a comparative study of the beginnings of prose fiction in Europe will make it clear how surprisingly mature is Lull's masterpiece of romances, *Blanquerna*, and how high a place in the early history of the novel must, on his account, be given to Catalonia.

We have no thought of comparing Lull, as others have done, and none too happily, with Dante, or making claims for him on the literary side which his Catalan works do not bear out fully. These may safely be left to speak for themselves, for in the last hundred years they have won a secure place in European literature. The point at issue here is that this aspect of Lull's genius was for centuries not apparent. Men wrangled over his theological terminology, and vainly endeavoured to defend or overthrow philosophical works which the progress of thought had already condemned to oblivion. They could not see that Ramon was first and foremost the Fool of Love—a man of intuition, a poet.

2. If Lull's position as a patriarch of Catalan literature has made him a hero in Catalonia, how much more have his character and life-story made him beloved of the whole Christian world! His personality is in all his writings, and to find it the reader tolerates their length and their repetitions, and is rewarded. The suggestion has been made that, in the controversies which raged round those writings, it was Lull's life and character that gave eternal vigour to his defenders rather than any inspiration to be found in the works themselves, or any faith in their future. It is certainly not his writings which have made him a missionary hero among English-speaking peoples, for until thirty years ago his English biographers knew practically nothing about them. It may not be out of place to add that the publication in English of the *Book of the Lover and the Beloved* has brought its translator letters from all over the world, from men and women of different religions, races and even colours, and that these correspondents have as a rule remarked less upon the book's content than upon the personality which lies behind it and even upon the over-brief biographical sketch of Ramon Lull which forms its preface.

It is not his achievements during a long and troubled
lifetime that have made him so compelling a figure. In the
practical sphere, for various reasons, he achieved very little.
Not, as has been sometimes suggested, because his temperament was one of impotent restlessness, but partly because
he spent himself as instinct, rather than reason, prompted
him, and partly—chiefly, indeed—because he flourished at
a time when ambitions clashed continually in political and
religious spheres, when idealism was waning fast and when
constructive idealists, in particular, had almost disappeared
from Europe. As Ramon's activities began, in his late
maturity, to quicken, the dead hand of the fourteenth
century was already about to fall upon the Continent—that
century in which " heresies and schisms grew apace, false
prophets . . . abounded, fierce wars . . . bathed half
Europe in blood, . . . religious orders decayed or followed
but weakly in the footsteps of their founders, great
theologians were dumb, and art degenerated almost wholly
into satire ".[1] Was it Lull's fault, we may ask, that
Aragon, France, Majorca and Sicily were continually em-
broiled in warfare? That the papacy was near its ebb, and
successive popes reigned but a few short years without the
necessary tranquillity, and sometimes without the disposition, to carry out reforms which Lull was not alone in
pressing? That the vitality which inspired the Crusades
had come to an end, that the military orders had declined,
that the king in whom Ramon centred his affection, trust
and expectations was by force of circumstances prevented
from carrying out his plans as the Conqueror might have
done? To these and other such causes Ramon owed the
checks which met him at every turn : in other days—either
earlier or later—he might have turned failure into brilliant
success.

[1] *R.L.*, p. 413, n. 3.

And yet, had he done so, the primary inspiration of his
life and character would be precisely what it is at the
present day. He has given us in himself an attractive
figure, which, by virtue of the romantic, the picturesque and
the poetical in it, makes an appeal to many whom the figure
of the recluse, the philosopher, the contemplative, would
never touch. To these—laymen, for the most part, like himself—he has shown what is meant by conversion, renunciation and love. He has shown them how a resolute spirit
can triumph over weakness and temptation, find its nourish-
ment in hardship, and win its satisfaction by sacrifice and
martyrdom. He has shown them what to a soul fired with
love, that "wearies not nor is wearied", is meant by a life
devoted wholly to the service of God, that spends and is
spent, toiling ceaselessly and joyfully with all its powers,
with its mind, soul and strength. Is it too much to say that,
while the greatest contemplatives endeavour to picture for
us the joys of the fruition of God in Heaven, this con-
templative-active, so like ourselves yet so different, has
given us some foretaste of the joys of those who spend
themselves in worship, yet are never spent, who "rest not
day and night, saying Holy, holy, holy, Lord God Almighty,
which was, and is, and is to come "?

3. If it is as an active that Ramon appeals to the present
age most widely, he appeals most deeply, and less obviously,
as a contemplative. It is a narrow criticism that, by any
criterion of mysticism, rejects him as a mystical writer:
though he does not, like many mystics, distinguish states,
degrees and steps of love, his *Book of the Lover and the
Beloved* is full of references to the Mystic Way and derives
from it all its power. Nor could we deny him the personal
title of mystic without ignoring the testimony of all his
biographers. The remembrance of a Pauline conversion,
of a supernatural inspiration, of Divine encouragement is

never lost, even by a writer given little to introspection
and spiritual autobiography; and because Ramon trans-
planted a flower that is wont to grow in monastic cells into
the very centre and heart of a troubled world, there are
few lovers of flowers who will be in danger of passing it
over.

What Sabatier says of St. Francis may be said equally
well of this Franciscan tertiary. He is " of the race of
mystics, for no intermediary comes between God and his
soul"; but his mysticism is patterned on the example " of
Jesus leading His disciples to the Tabor of contemplation ".
When they would fain stay there, he leads them down to
the crowds and the plain.[1] And this in two senses, for Lull
leads his readers down from Randa's heights, both to the
busy, peopled plain of active endeavour and to the abstract
desert of his own arid philosophy.

This comparison can be extended very widely, for the
Majorcan martyr, first and greatest of Franciscan tertiaries
in that island, is in many ways most like to the best-loved
of medieval saints. Not only does everything spell love
to him but he can express his ideals both quaintly and
sublimely :

> . . . Whatever talk thou hear,
> Whatever music, anywhere,
> Joglar or clerk, or bird in air,
> The roaring of tumultuous seas,
> The wind that murmurs in the trees:
> Love God, I say, in all of these.[2]

He possessed in an unusual degree what the *Fioretti*
speaks of as "that celestial virtue whereby all earthly
things and transitory are trodden under foot and every

[1] *R.L.*, p. 416, n. 5.   [2] *R.L.*, p. 417, n. 2.

barrier is removed which might hinder the soul from freely uniting itself to the eternal God ".[1] No more than St. Francis can he be imagined as identifying contemplation with inactivity. " His conclusion was that which was evidenced by his life; that the highest life which it is possible to lead is one in which the strength and the power to be effectively active in the outer world are gained in the mysteries of contemplation. Activity without contemplation may be both holy and effective, contemplation without activity may be equally holy and . . . even more effective, but it is the combination of both by which the effectiveness and the holiness are raised to their highest power."[2]

Any Franciscan who reads the *Book of Contemplation*, *Blanquerna*, or the finest of Lull's poems will recognize in them the fashion of the master-hand. St. Francis desired that his followers should be " jongleurs of the Lord ": in Ramon Lull he had one who delighted in that name, or rather in those which he himself preferred—the " joglar " and the " Fool " of love. St. Francis' writings were as scant as Lull's were voluminous, but there are striking similarities, both in substance and in style, between them. In many passages of St. Francis we seem to hear the words of his follower, while parts of Ramon's paraphrase of the Lord's Prayer in the *Art of Contemplation* bear a marked resemblance to the paraphrase made by St. Francis. All the apt phrases with which Fr. Paschal Robinson characterizes St. Francis can be applied to Ramon the Fool as exactly as though they had been written of him: his combination, for example, of " great elevation of thought " with " picturesqueness of expression " and his " deep sense of the spiritual " clothed " with the spirit of romance ". Or two other phrases which, true enough of St. Francis, go far towards summing up the character of Ramon:

[1] *Fioretti*, Chap. 13 (tr. Arnold).   [2] *R.L.*, p. 417, n. 4.

He was at once formidably mystic and exquisitely human.
He had the soul of an ascetic and the heart of a poet.[1]

There, then, we have the Ramon Lull of to-day—and,
we may safely predict, of a space of time extending far into
the future.   A patriarch of literature, an apostle of religion,
and a herald among the mystics.   The part of his work
which was never destined to be immortal is dead already,
and has the interest but of the mummy of a Pharaoh.   The
part which will live is now, after six centuries, achieving
a new degree of popularity.   "Thy wings are eagle's
wings," wrote Verdaguer, one of the leaders of the Catalan
Renaissance, "but thy sweet song is the nightingale's."
And the Nicaraguan, Rubén Darío, took up the picturesque
phrase as he caught the music of the nightingales singing
"among the oaks of his philosophy".   That music, once
drowned amid the clamour of the Schools, is unlikely to
vanish again.

Even after another six centuries, though many of the
works described in this biography may be buried in
oblivion, it is difficult to see how the name of Ramon Lull
can be lost.   Even if the virile tongue of Catalonia should
be silenced, the apostle and the herald will outlive the
patriarch.   Reduce the bulk of Lull's writings, by the fiercest
flames of criticism, to ashes, and there still remain *Blanquerna*, and a collection of fragments, unharmed.   For
these defy criticism and transcend argument; and, while a
spark of love for God remains in a human soul, it is unthink-
able that Ramon's sublime hymns of love can ever perish.

[1] *R.L.*, p. 418, nn. 1-4.

INDEX

James II, King of Catalonia-Aragon, 81-2, 86, 102, 103

James II, King of Majorca, 10, 11, 15, 21, 33, 34, 37, 38, 76, 81, 86, 100, 117

Jerusalem, 85

Jewish faith, 24

Jews, treatment of (by Christians), 82

joglar, the, 26, 28, 41, 119, 120

John XXI, Pope, 37

jongleur, *v. joglar*

Kalila and Dimna, 60

kings and their subjects, relations between, 27-8

Korân, 56

language teaching, *v.* colleges

Languedoc, 46

law, Ramon Lull and, 97

Leo X, Pope, 108

Liber (or *Libellus*) *de Fine*, 84-5, 86

Llobet, Joan, 110

Louis, St., 10

Luanco, José Ramón, 114

Lull, Ramon. LIFE. Early life, 9-10. Amorous adventures, 10-12. Conversion, 12 - 14. Studies, 15 - 16. Second conversion, 16-18. Life in Palma, 18 - 20. Randa and Miramar, 31-6. Travels, 37. Perpignan and Montpellier, 36-8. Rome, 56. Paris, 57-8. Montpellier, 62. Spiritual crisis in Genoa, 62 - 3. First African mission, 63 - 5. Naples and Rome, 66-8,

Lull's life—*continued*
75. Professes as a Franciscan tertiary, 74. Paris: combats with Averroists, 76 - 7. Barcelona and Majorca, 82. Cyprus, 83. Further travels in Europe, 83-7. Paris: encounter with Duns Scotus, 87. Second African mission, 87 - 92. Shipwreck and stay in Pisa, 92-3. Movement for a new crusade, 94-6. Last journey to Paris, 96-7. Council of Vienne, 97-9. Majorca, 99-100. Makes his will, 100-2. Third African mission, 102 - 4. Death, 104. Burial, 105

WORKS. *V.* titles of works, *passim*

CHARACTER. Fool of love, 45, 62, 66, 72, 88, 103, 116, 120. Personality, 116-18. Thoroughness, 9, 10. Easy disposition, 10. Practical idealism, 14-15, 16. Volatility, 15, 63, 86. Energy, 21, 38, 75, 92, 118. Ruling passion, 28, 30. Robustness and vitality, 72 - 3. Reasons for the slightness of his achievements, 117

POSTHUMOUS HISTORY. Beginnings of Lullian cult, 106. Campaign against Lullism, 106-7. Revived vogue in sixteenth century, 107-8. Reaction in eighteenth century, 108-9.